Let the Oppressed Go Free

Gender and the Biblical Tradition

Mary Magdalene at the tomb.
Copyright © 1992 Pem Pfisterer Clark.

Let the Oppressed Go Free

Feminist Perspectives on the New Testament

Luise Schotroff

Translated by
Annemarie S. Kidder

Westminster/John Knox Press
Louisville, Kentucky

© 1991 Christian Kaiser Verlag
English translation © 1993 Westminster/John Knox Press

All rights reserved. No part of this book may be reproduced in any form or by any means, electronic or mechanical, including photocopying, recording, or by any information storage or retrieval system, without permission in writing from the publisher. For information, address Westminster/John Knox Press, 100 Witherspoon Street, Louisville, Kentucky 40202-1396.

This volume was originally published in slightly different form in 1991 under the title *Befreiungserfahrungen* by Christian Kaiser Verlag, Munich, Germany.

Unless marked otherwise, scripture quotations are from the New Revised Standard Version of the Bible, copyright © 1989 by the Division of Christian Education of the National Council of the Churches of Christ in the U.S.A., and are used by permission.

Frontispiece artwork is copyright © 1992 by Pem Pfisterer Clark and is used by permission.

Book design by Ken Taylor

First edition

Published by Westminster/John Knox Press
Louisville, Kentucky

This book is printed on recycled acid-free paper that meets the American National Standards Institute Z39.48 standard. ∞

PRINTED IN THE UNITED STATES OF AMERICA

9 8 7 6 5 4 3 2 1

Library of Congress Cataloging-in-Publication Data

Schottroff, Luise.
   [Befreiungserfahrungen. English. Selections]
   Let the oppressed go free : Feminist perspectives on the New Testament / Luise Schottroff.
      p.   cm.—(Gender and the biblical tradition)
   Selections from the author's Befreiungserfahrungen.
   Includes index.
   Contents: Experiences of liberation—How justified is the feminist critique of Paul?—"Leaders of the faith" (or "just some pious womenfolk")?—Women as disciples of Jesus in New Testament times—Lydia, a new quality of power — The woman who loved much and the Pharisee Simon (Luke 7:36-50)—The virgin birth (Luke 1:26-33, 38)—Mary Magdalene and the women at Jesus' tomb.
   ISBN 0-664-25426-8 (pbk.: alk. paper)

1. Women in the Bible.   2. Women in Christianity—History—Early church, ca. 30-600.   3. Bible. N.T.—Criticism, interpretation, etc.   4. Feminist theology.   5. Liberation theology.   6. Sociology, Biblical.   I. Title.   II. Series.
BS2445.S3762513   1993
225.6'082—dc20   92-33116

Contents

Foreword, by Elisabeth Schüssler Fiorenza	7
Preface	11
Abbreviations	19
1. Experiences of Liberation: Freedom and Liberation According to Biblical Evidence	21
2. How Justified Is the Feminist Critique of Paul?	35
3. "Leaders of the Faith" or "Just Some Pious Womenfolk"?	60
4. Women as Disciples of Jesus in New Testament Times	80
5. Lydia: A New Quality of Power	131
6. The Woman Who Loved Much and the Pharisee Simon (Luke 7:36–50)	138
7. The Virgin Birth (Luke 1:26–33, 38)	158
8. Mary Magdalene and the Women at Jesus' Tomb	168
Scripture Index	204

EDITOR'S NOTE

The author cites numerous modern scholarly works in German, and we regret that the references to translations are inconsistent. At times a corresponding page number in an English version could be supplied. At other times only a corresponding English title is provided along with the German references. Occasionally German works cited may exist in English translations we were unable to locate.

Foreword

Luise Schottroff and I met for the first time in 1979 at an international colloquium on apocalypticism that was held in Uppsala, Sweden. I had long admired her work on Gnosticism and was looking forward very much to meeting her since she was the foremost German woman scholar in biblical studies. If I had anticipated a discussion on Gnostic dualism, I would have been disappointed. She told me from the outset that she had lost interest in the kind of history-of-religions approach that always ended up attempting to prove that the position of the "orthodox" early Christian writer was the right one. The comparative history-of-religion approach of her teachers, R. Bultmann and H. Braun, she argued, not only tended to use the position of the "others" as a foil for Christian self-understanding but also devalued "other religions" of the New Testament, Greco-Roman cultural environment.

However, Luise spoke glowingly of an exegetical working group in Heidelberg to which she and Willi Schottroff belonged. This circle of biblical scholars sought to pioneer a social-history method to biblical interpretation that could overcome the history-of-ideas approach that determined hegemonic biblical scholarship in the past and still does so today.[1] I knew that the so-called materialist interpretation of the Bible had made some inroads into left-wing European biblical circles, and I was aware that it found only a cool and belated reception in the North American academy. Yet, I had not heard of this scholarly Heidelberg group and its methodological approach. Therefore I was looking forward eagerly to reading their first collection of essays aptly entitled *Der Gott der kleinen Leute*,[2] which had just appeared.

Luise Schottroff also spoke of the increasing problems she faced trying to get her new work published in established German exegetical journals. I shared with her my own very positive experience with American editorial boards but pointed to a recent negative episode with German Catholic scholars. They had refused to publish a research paper on the reconstruction of early Christian history from a critical feminist perspective that I had been invited to give at a scholarly symposium celebrating the sixty-fifth birthday of the distinguished biblical scholar Rudolf Schnackenburg, my thesis adviser.[3] Although at that time Luise Schottroff seemed to share the German leftist misunderstanding of feminism as just a movement of white, middle-class women, she promised that she would look at the paper and see whether her Heidelberg working group would publish it. She made good on her word, and in 1980 my paper appeared in a collection of essays entitled *Frauen in der Bibel* to which Luise herself contributed the essay "Women as Disciples of Jesus in New Testament Times." Her social-historical feminist work documented in this book had been launched.

I am grateful to Westminster/John Knox Press for making this significant research available to a wide North American audience. Indeed, one of the distinguishing characteristics of Luise Schottroff's work is her interest in communicating her biblical scholarship in language accessible to a wide audience. I am certain that in North America her book will attract a great number of readers committed to Christian community and/or the feminist movement just as it has done in her native Germany.

These essays, however, are of equally great interest to biblical studies in general and feminist biblical scholarship in particular. They not only introduce the feminist social-historical method that Luise Schottroff has developed. They also contribute to North American feminist debates on whether scholars should abandon historical reconstruction in favor of literary and ideological criticism. Luise clearly believes that it is possible to move beyond the androcentric text to the life-situation not just of first-century elite women but also of those who were most exploited by Roman imperial patriarchal structures. Both of these moves—her historical-political "class" analysis and her hermeneutical option to make poor and lowly people historically visible and present—introduce a distinctive element into North American hegemonic and feminist biblical discourses. Most importantly, her careful inquiry into hitherto neglected areas of historical research unearths a wealth of social-historical information that makes early Christian women come alive as people who are quite different from us but yet still remain very familiar to us. In this book our Jewish and Christian forebears of faith receive voice and historical agency.

Elisabeth Schüssler Fiorenza

Notes

1. For documentation of this development see her article "How My Mind Has Changed, oder: Neutestamentliche Wissenschaft im Dienste von Befreiung," *EvT* 48 (1988): 247–61.

2. A selection of these essays was published under the title *The God of the Lowly: Socio-historical Interpretations of the Bible* (Maryknoll, N.Y.: Orbis Books, 1984).

3. This essay was published in English as "You Are Not to Be Called Father: Early Christian History in a Feminist Perspective," *Cross Currents* 29 (1979): 301–19.

Preface

The exegetical studies contained in this volume have been formulated since 1980 as contributions to the development of feminist liberation theology in my context—the German Federal Republic. I shall leave it up to the readers to determine in what way they are relevant for the context of North America. I shall be glad to receive any response. I have developed these studies in dialogues with men and women who, as I am, are engaged in the feminist and peace movements. Until recently, Germany has been divided by a border. Both sides were saturated by atomic weapons and by hatred for the other side. Yet even today, after the unification, one needs to do work, in line with the Sermon on the Mount, against militarism and for peace in Europe. Through the conflicts that resulted from my efforts in the peace movement in the day-to-day work of my profession—as professor of New Testament at a university—I have come to realize how deep are the roots of sexism and oppression of women in our culture, theology, and institutions. I have come to understand how militarism, oppression of women, class rule, destruction of nature, and racism are related in their substance. Together with Elisabeth Schüssler Fiorenza and other feminist female scholars, I now use the term "patriarchy" to designate the material interconnectedness of oppressive structures that are mutually supportive.[1]

In the course of the last ten years, it has become more and more clear to me that, through my work,

I should like to overcome the separations so common in our culture: the separation of scholarship and life, the separation of theology and everyday experiences, the separation of worship and political grass-roots work. Therefore, the studies of this volume try to hold together various levels, mainly the level of Christian practice in the social context and that of scholarly theology.

I have tried to develop a scholarly point of departure in social history for the study of the New Testament. The goal of this perspective is to explore and visualize the oppression of women and the economic exploitation and political oppression of all people. I have tried to reconstruct as concretely as possible the living conditions of women in early Christian communities in order to find out what constituted the liberating practice of women and men back then. I have dealt with early Christianity at the time of Jesus in Palestine as at the time of the early communities in other Roman provinces up to the end of the first century as a liberation movement of women and men within the oppressive system of the so-called Pax Romana.[2] The oppression of women was an explicit and relevant aspect of the Roman rule. Hence, I have tried not to simply add the history of women to the history of men but to trace the oppression of women and the liberation of women within the overall social structure of patriarchy. This scholarly point of departure of a feminist social history stands, and stood, in dialogue—also in critical dialogue—with the peace and feminist movements of my own context.[3]

In all this, I have not considered the New Testament as a norm for today's Christian practice; instead, I have regarded the liberating actions and the faith of the people standing behind the texts of the New Testament as an encouragement and inspiration for today's hard path to justice, peace, and the integrity of creation. The final goal of this path is quite comprehensive. It comprises a worldwide process of healing, yet I can walk the path only from here, from my own place of origin, from my homeland, which is a so-called first-world country.

The first steps on this path are difficult because most of our theological traditions are not interested in such goals but, instead, are concerned with only the preservation of the existing order. A further difficulty is the prevalent perception of scholars—and even of theological scholars—that if their scholarship is less involved with the life and everyday experiences of people of today, then that scholarship will be all the more neutral, objective, and "correct." Without a fundamental critique of theological and academic methods and traditions, it is impossible to find a way for the liberation of women and men from the power structures sustained with the help of Christianity. Hence, I try to conduct and explain this critique in these essays also.

Because my point of departure for a feminist social history of the New Testament is based on the praxis context of liberation movements, I have been prompted to present my scholarly work in a way as intelligible to the general public as possible. I have also regularly presented my exegetical work to the church's public, as, for example, at the Deutscher Evangelischer Kirchentag (a nationwide event of study and celebration sponsored by the German Protestant churches). The scholarly essays in this volume are written in such a way that interested laypersons should also be able to follow them.

The essays published in this volume are a selection from my anthology *Befreiungserfahrungen: Studien zur Sozialgeschichte des Neuen Testaments*.[4] In the selection presented here, the first essay reflects on the liberation-theological terms "freedom" and "liberation" in the context of the Bible. The second essay is located within the discussion of the critique of Paul on the part of feminist and liberation movements. In their justified anger with the arch-patriarchal picture of Paul promulgated by the church, these movements see a connection between the historical Paul and the Paul that the conservative history of dealing with his texts has produced. By their anger, however, members of these movements deprive themselves of the supports Paul could give for a liberating practice today, in spite of those texts of his that subjugate women. The third essay is situated in the discussion of anti-Judaism in feminist theology and tries to show from historical material that the general view of Jewish religion as antiwomen is incorrect.[5] The fourth essay attempts to draw an overall picture of the situation of women in early Christianity within the social reality, conveyed by social history, of women's lives in the Roman Empire. It is especially important to me here to distinguish between the women of the upper class and of the poor population; the poor were the majority, and the first Christians were a part of that group. The fifth essay highlights a feminist social-historical key experience of mine: the insight, based on historical studies concerning the profession of a seller of purple fabrics, that Lydia was not a well-to-do woman, as exegetical tradition tells us and as I, too, had long believed, but rather was a laborer in a lowly profession. The sixth essay shows how much attention the Jesus tradition pays to the working world of women who are prostitutes; it also deals with the fact that this tradition does perceive the world of prostitutes in a loving—and not a moralizing—way. The seventh essay criticizes theological tradition with its antiwomen concept concerning virginity and divine conception, and it tries to reinterpret the biblical text (Luke 1:26–33, 38) in new ways.

The final, eighth essay shows through extrabiblical material that the women at the cross took a great political risk when showing solidarity with a crucified person. This essay describes ancestral Christian sisters on their journey to justice, a justice the Roman officials wanted to extinguish by means of crucifixions.

My work is and was connected with two groups of scholars, to whom I am indebted. Since 1978, the Heidelberg Working Group for Social-Historical Biblical Exegesis has been an important circle for joint discussion not only of historical detail but also of mutual spiritual experiences.[6] The Kassel Groupings on Research on Feminist Liberation Theology has tied my work closely to a large group of women, who in this scholarly context analyze their experiences and reflect on them from a feminist liberation-theological viewpoint. Both groups hold that Christian faith needs to be understood mainly as the practice of faith in *everyday life*. Subjects discussed in the Kassel Groupings since 1987 include: guilt and power, patriarchy, and women and money.[7] In these groupings, women conduct work projects after academic research has been done on the subject matter. The results of this research are then reevaluated and critically developed. And it is in this context also that feminist theological dissertations are written. I am grateful to all the women who have supported my work in this respect, and I am especially grateful to Christine Schaumberger.

Furthermore, I am grateful to Westminster/John Knox Press; to Dr. Karen King, who served as a reader of the work; and to Cynthia Thompson, my editor; all have paved the way for the publication of these essays in English. I thank Dr. Annemarie S. Kidder for her translation into English and Dr. Martin Rumscheidt for his extensive support and advice.

Notes

1. E. Schüssler Fiorenza, *In Memory of Her: A Feminist Theological Reconstruction of Christian Origins* (New York: Crossroad, 1983).
2. See on that L. Schottroff and W. Stegemann, *Jesus and the Hope of the Poor* (Maryknoll, N.Y.: Orbis Books, 1986).
3. For a detailed account, see L. Schottroff, "How My Mind Has Changed, oder: Neutestamentliche Wissenschaft im Dienste von Befreiung," *EvT* 48 (1988): 247–61.
4. L. Schottroff, *Befreiungserfahrungen: Studien zur Sozialgeschichte des Neuen Testaments* (Munich, 1990).
5. Anti-Judaism in feminist theology is not a particular problem of feminist theology but is rather part of the anti-Judaism of Christian theology at large, to whose analysis I pay constant attention; see, for example, ibid., 324–57.
6. Publications of the Heidelberg Working Group are, for example: W. Schottroff and W. Stegemann, eds., *Der Gott der kleinen Leute*, 2 vols. (Munich, 1979); a selection thereof in English translation, *God of the Lowly: Socio-historical Interpretations of the Bible* (Maryknoll, N.Y.: Orbis Books, 1984); L. Schottroff and W. Schottroff, eds., *Mitarbeiter der Schöpfung: Bibel und Arbeitswelt* (Munich, 1983); L. Schottroff and W. Schottroff, eds., *Wer ist unser Gott? Beiträge zu einer Befreiungstheologie im Kontext der "ersten" Welt* (Munich, 1986).
7. Some publications of the Kassel Groupings on Research on Feminist Liberation Theology are: C. Schaumberger, ed., *Weil wir nicht vergessen wollen: Zu einer Feministischen Theologie im deutschen Kontext*, Anfragen: Diskussionen Feministischer Theologie 1 (Münster, 1987); C. Schaumberger and L. Schottroff, *Schuld und Macht: Studien zu einer feministischen Befreiungstheologie* (Munich, 1988); C. Schaumberger, "Es geht um jede

Minute unseres Lebens! Auf dem Weg zu einer kontextuellen feministischen Befreiungstheologie," in R. Jost and U. Kubera, eds., *Befreiung hat viele Farben: Feministische Theologie als kontextuelle Befreiungstheologie* (Gütersloh, 1991), 15–34; L. Schottroff, "DienerInnen der Heiligen: Der Diakonat der Frauen im Neuen Testament," in G. K. Schäfer and T. Strohm, eds., *Diakonie—biblische Grundlagen und Orientierungen* (Heidelberg, 1990), 222–42; L. Schottroff, "Wanderprophetinnen: Eine feministische Analyse der Logienquelle," *EvT* 51 (1991): 332–44; English translation, "Itinerant Prophetesses: A Feminist Analysis of the Sayings Source Q," *Occasional Papers of the Institute for Antiquity and Christianity* 21 (1991); L. Schottroff et al., eds., *Wörterbuch der Feministischen Theologie* (Gütersloh, 1991).

Abbreviations

Ann.	*Annales* (Tacitus)
Ant.	*Jewish Antiquities* (Josephus)
BJ	*Bellum Judaicum* (Josephus)
BK	*Bibel und Kirche*
BZ	*Biblische Zeitschrift*
EKKNT	Evangelisch-katholischer Kommentar zum Neuen Testament
EvT	*Evangelische Theologie*
ExpTim	*Expository Times*
HAW	Handbuch der Altertumswissenschaft, München
HNT	Handbuch zum Neuen Testament
HTKNT	Herders theologischer Kommentar zum Neuen Testament
JAAR	*Journal of the American Academy of Religion*
JJS	*Journal of Jewish Studies*
MGWJ	*Monatsschrift für Geschichte und Wissenschaft des Judentums*
NTD	Das Neue Testament Deutsch
NTS	*New Testament Studies*

PW	Pauly-Wissowa, *Real-Encyclopädie der classischen Altertumswissenschaft*
PWSup	Supplement to PW
RAC	*Reallexikon für Antike und Christentum*
RGG	*Die Religion in Geschichte und Gegenwart*
SBLDS	Society of Biblical Literature Dissertation Series
SBS	Stuttgarter Bibelstudien
TDNT	G. Kittel and G. Friedrich (eds.), *Theological Dictionary of the New Testament*
THKNT	Theologischer Handkommentar zum Neuen Testament
TQ	*Theologische Quartalschrift*
TWNT	G. Kittel and G. Friedrich (eds.), *Theologisches Wörterbuch zum Neuen Testament;* English translations in *TDNT*
USQR	*Union Seminary Quarterly Review*
ZAW	*Zeitschrift für die alttestamentliche Wissenschaft*
ZKT	*Zeitschrift für katholische Theologie*
ZNW	*Zeitschrift für die neutestamentliche Wissenschaft*

1

Experiences of Liberation: Freedom and Liberation According to Biblical Evidence

Bondage

The word "freedom" is rooted historically in one of the most gruesome inventions of human history, which itself is not exactly void of brutality: It was that those who let others, people in bondage (slaves), work for them called themselves "free" (full citizens). The slaves, who were in bondage in the legal sense, were in the free people's eyes "living possessions," "tools." Since we, the free, cannot do without slave labor, it must have been ordained by nature, says Aristotle, thus formulating the self-perception of the free in the societies of antiquity (*Po-*

litica 1252a.30; 1253b). The reality of the lives of slaves is realistically described by the Gospels' parables on slaves. Although slaves do not suffer from hunger since the owner has an interest in their labor, their everyday lives are determined by experiences of violence. They are tortured, beaten, and murdered; even among themselves, there is violence: Slaves fight with each other and tell on their fellow slaves before their master (Matt. 18:31; 21:35-36; 22:6; 24:51; Luke 12:45).

The Bible describes, apart from the bondage of the slaves, the bondage of the farming community and the political bondage of entire peoples—as it corresponds to the social reality of its time. The farming population in Palestine at the time Christianity evolves is, though not enslaved in the legal sense, oppressed through indebtedness. The situation of the many debtors unable to pay and the ensuing violence on their creditors' part is a continually repeated scene, which is the terror of many people (see, e.g., Neh. 5:1-5; Luke 12:58-59). It is no coincidence that the meaning of God's "forgiveness" is depicted in terms of this situation: God forgives; that is, God remits debts (see Matt. 6:12; 18:23-35). The indebted small farmer is facing the forfeiture of his clothes, the sale of his family, debtor's arrest, debtor's slavery, indigence, illness, or the life of a day laborer, who has to endure extended periods of unemployment. The picture offered by the Gospels concerning the situation of the farming population is true to life and, in many instances, matches secular sources. The political bondage of entire peoples is given a clear name in the New Testament: "You know that... the rulers lord it over their subjects, and... make them feel the weight of authority" (Mark 10:42 par.; NEB).

Romans 13:1-7 is part of a long chain of declarations of loyalty on the part of oppressed nations toward their political overlords. As in Rom. 13:1-7, Christians, Jews, and other politically oppressed had to declare their loyalty to, for example, the Romans, knowing all along that political conflict was unavoidable as long as they placed their own God above the gods of the political masters.

Both Plato and Aristotle talk, as most of the educated of antiquity, about freedom from the perspective of the "free," the wealthy, and the political masters. Biblical tradition, however, talks *from the perspective of those at the bottom.* Here, it is not the free or the Stoic philosophers who are talking about their station in life or inner freedom. Instead, three horizons of experience from the perspective of the afflicted are present, namely those of slavery, impoverishment and indebtedness, and political oppression. It is no coincidence that one finds no biblical analogies to Aristotle's view described above. The idea of an inner freedom that is possible even apart from any external conditions—an idea found, for example, in Seneca (*De beneficiis* 3.20.1)—is not a biblical thought and cannot be found even in Paul, though some interpreters (e.g., J. Weiss) of 1 Cor. 7:21ff. have argued otherwise. The idea of an inner freedom independent from people's reality of life, where they suffer hunger or are slaves or are wealthy, has its origin where a rich upper class finds its political scope of action restricted (see Seneca). In the Bible, however, the voices of those who are marked by the experiences of bondage are heard.

The Bible consistently views bondage—just as freedom—in the holistic sense of the word. The New Testament word "body" (*sōma*) expresses this holistic aspect: Bondage is a bodily, psychological, social, and religious reality; all areas of human identity are involved, and even hopes are crushed (see Rom. 6:12–14). Inner and outer conditions are not separated, and the bodily afflictions caused by bondage are described in detail (see, e.g., 1 Cor. 4:11–13 or the descriptions of Christ's passion— his death parallels the execution of many who are in a similar situation).

Bondage, in all its dimensions, is not described in a value-free manner, but is clearly named for what it is. Political oppression is considered horrible (see the formulations of Mark 10:42, above). Paul also assumes that Roman rule is unjust, though instituted by God. The violent rule of masters over slaves, of Greeks over barbarians, and of men over women is unjust in the eyes of God—that is the clear implication of Gal. 3:28 and 1 Cor. 12:13. Further, the parables in the Gospels that compare God to a creditor or rich landowner do not side with the creditor or landowner but illustrate the wrath of God. People who have dealt with their neighbor without pity stand before a wrathful God in the same way as the debtor who is unable to pay stands before the creditor, who now has the trembling little man in his hand. The world experienced by slaves, tenants, and day laborers as oppressive lies open to God's wrath. Everyday experiences of social reality show that as regards the human dimension, God's creation is in ruin.

It is important to recognize that the Bible's portrayal of bondage comes from *the perspective of the escaped*. The exodus from slavery in Egypt becomes the heart and central experience of God to a people that, in times of renewed oppression, finds sustenance in remembering the liberation of long ago (Deut. 15:15; 24:18, 22; etc.). In the New Testament, too, oppression is described from the perspective of liberation and is recognized in its overall structure only because of this. Only as a freed person, inhabited by the Spirit of God, can Paul say how hard it was to live under the bondage of sin (Rom. 7:25; 8:1). The gospel of the poor, which is the fulfillment of God's promise (Isa. 61:1) according to Jesus' understanding and that of the Jesus movement, causes the kind of liberation that enables people to recognize the vast destruction caused by poverty. It is not only hunger, lament, and disease but also the inability to praise God that crushes the poor to the ground, so that they are poor to the core, "in spirit" (Matt. 5:3).

According to the Bible's understanding, bondage is found, as we have seen, mainly in the three areas: oppression of slaves, of debtors, and of peoples. Yet beyond these areas, one detects a clear sensibility for the brutality in which people rule over people, as well as for the violence found in men's relationship to women. The power structures are viewed here from the perspective of the afflicted; they are recognized in their overall form—that is, holistically—and are despised as an injustice before God. Biblical tradition describes bondage in this radical way because those afflicted by it have already, in part, experienced liberation—they are standing already with one foot on liberated territory.

The Jesus Movement: God's Reign as Process of Liberation

We meet the word "freedom" (*eleutheria*) and its derivatives in the Synoptic Gospels only on the margins (see Matt. 17:26). However, it is still reasonable to use the word "liberation" in the translation and the clarification of other words, as, for example, the word for forgiveness or remission (*aphesis*), denoting the remission of debts, the setting free of captives, and God's forgiveness. "Beatitude" depicts liberation also, just as the word "gospel" (*evangelion*) does. The good news means that the plight of the poor is coming to an end. Beatitude is not only a promise for the future but brings about the beginning of God's rule already in the present (see Matt. 5:3–4 par., together with Matt. 11:5 par.). For that reason, one needs to interpret the term "reign of God" itself as liberation; also, one needs to understand the story of Jesus and his followers in New Testament times not only as a story of those proclaiming liberation, but also as a story of the praxis of liberation in which other people besides Jesus were involved and which lived on after his death.

The fact that God is ruler, that God is the ruler of all creation, means liberation already now: "No one can serve two masters.... You cannot serve God and mammon" (Matt. 6:24). God's reign ends the oppression caused by the rule of people and their gods, of which mammon is one; God's rule is the force of the mightier one against the forces that deliver people into bondage. Oppression by political masters is on the same level—is just as dangerous and far-reaching—as oppression by demons.

The liberating praxis brought about by Jesus meant that people gathered to form a community. From the very start, Jesus' followers formed such communities, lived together, and traveled the country together. The report of Acts 2:42–47 concerning the early Christian community in Jerusalem after Jesus' resurrection most likely describes the basic elements of the community's development: praying and rejoicing together (see below), having meals together, sharing the scarce food supplies, healing the sick. The misery of disease was everywhere in the impoverished country. One could find the sick of Palestine's villages and cities in the marketplaces or at the public sacred places for the sick, such as at the Beth-zatha pool (John 5:4; Luke 10:9). Jesus and his followers healed the sick, and all those involved viewed the healings of the sick as the beginning of liberation of the entire nation. Jesus' liberating praxis spread at incredible speed. The whole nation was to be reached. Whoever was healed became at once both healer and prophet.

The new communities did not isolate themselves but were consistently active in addressing, in a public and intelligible manner, not only every individual person, but also entire cities and villages. The reign of God is an all-embracing goal because God is both lord and master of the entire world. This goal furnished the practical modes of behavior of the people following Jesus. Even the conflicts resulting from the praxis of liberation were endured because the eyes of Jesus' followers were on the all-embracing goal. The believers announced that anyone committing injustices against God and people would soon be judged by God. But the announcement of the judgment left punishment up to God. All enemies of Jesus' message were to be won over precisely by confronting them very clearly with the will of God. Perhaps, they would turn back after all (Matt. 5:44ff.).

The difficulties that had to be overcome by the Jesus movement and by Jesus were great, and, in the same way as Jesus, many of Jesus' followers were killed because of their work. It was hard on all involved to endure the warranted fear. The passion story in the Gospel of Mark clearly depicts this fear. All disciples have fled (Mark 14:50) because they had to fear that, as Jesus' followers, they too would be arrested and crucified the same way as Jesus. Some of the leaders of the Jewish people cooperated with the Romans, who were the actual political leaders. Their goal was to subdue any unrest among the people right away. The Jesus movement was not a political movement since it did not have political goals (such as expelling the Romans from the country). However, the movement constituted a massive threat to Roman power due to its agenda to turn all people into children of God, who then would serve only God and no other master. The day could be foreseen when the people would look to God and no longer to mammon; when the people would no longer be weighed down and oppressed "like sheep without a shepherd" (Matt. 9:36).

The transformation of someone in bondage into a person in freedom meant becoming a child of God; in most cases, however, one spoke of becoming a *son* of God (see, e.g., Matt. 5:9, 45), in accordance with the androcentrism of the time. Being a son or child of God meant: no longer being the slave of other masters and forces, being able to love the other of God's children, and experiencing the joy of liberation as one's endowment with strength. Jesus' followers felt full of strength and victory, not small and insignificant. Numerous texts express this victorious self-understanding—for instance, the parable of the mustard seed (Mark 4:30–32 par.) and Mark 9:23, which says, "All things are possible to one who believes" (RSV). Being a child of God was another way of saying one was free. (On the relationship between being a child and being free, see, e.g., Matt. 17:26 and John 8:33, 35.)

Liberation from the Power of Sin

The terms "freedom" and "to free" are important to Paul. Paul's basic thesis is this: Christ's resurrection frees believers from the power of sin (see especially Rom. 6:18–22; 8:2). Unfortunately, the word "sin" produces, by today's standards and based on its effects in history, a moral-individualistic misunderstanding. According to Paul, however, sin is a world power; sin is a queen, ruling over all humanity and human history. The many small and great malicious things people do to each other (see the impressive list, e.g., in Rom. 1:29–32) add up to a collective system of coercion, which makes every single person subject to it. Thus, the person is sold out to sin, enslaved by sin, bonded to sin in every aspect of life, bringing death upon the self and upon all humanity. Romans 7:14–24 describes the desperate situation of a human race that has become the marionette of its collective self-destruction. Even the will of God, the Torah, which wants to bring life to people, becomes an instrument of the queen called sin. Sin uses the Torah against its very purpose, and, thus, the holy will of God actually seals people's death penalty since they are unable to live according to God's will. Christ's resurrection has done away with this rule of violence, Paul says. Sin's power has been broken, and people are able to live under Christ's protection and need no longer labor on behalf of death and destruction. Paul imagines the power of God and the power of Christ as a vast expanse in which one can live and under whose protection one can experience liberation from the power of sin in the transformation of one's whole life. (Paul indicates this experience, e.g., by saying we are "in Christ.")

Paul's ideas (and the actual lives of those who lived in the Christian communities of the time) are not too different from those of the Jesus movement as we know it through the Synoptic Gospels. It is an unacceptable procedure, as happens often, to list the terminological differences without cognizance of what they have in common in their practice. Here, too, it is important to note that the believers live in communities and that, in their process of liberation, they orient themselves on the aim of God's rule. Their behavior is governed by equality among each other, love within the community of faith, and a struggle for the people—every single one of them, with the goal of reaching them all.

The admonitions in Rom. 12:1–21 offer a good view on the nature of Christian life, on the "worship amidst the world's everyday life."[1] Also, Paul views here both Christ's and God's rule as a *counter*force. Liberation is submission to the greater counterforce, that of God. In Rom. 6:19, Paul even reflects on this thought with its offensiveness. It certainly is a problem to him why liberation appears—to put it bluntly—as a new form of slavery. He justifies this fact by saying that the enslavement by sin, which takes over the body, requires a counterforce ("just as... so now" in Rom. 6:19), which now readies the body for sanctification and for bearing fruit.

Paul's comments on slavery and on the role of women in the church have produced many uncertainties. In most cases, one insists with much idealism that Paul should have called for an end to slavery out of principle. Or, one argues that he considered external living conditions as marginal and said, for that reason, a slave should remain a slave. Both interpretations, particularly of 1 Cor. 7:21–22, do not do enough to imagine the living conditions at the time. Those legally in bondage were only one part of the exploited population; the broad proletariat of day laborers and those who had been set free, though enjoying freedom in the legal sense, were in reality exploited in other ways. It made good sense to the slave owner of the time to liberate slaves and then continue exploiting them in terms of services and financial payments. The distinctions of the bondage of slaves, of the liberated, and of day laborers (such as Paul himself) were only relative. Therefore, it is important to see that the change that slaves experienced in their condition upon entering Christian communities took place on the level of *practice*. In the churches, they had equal rights, and the churches took a stance on the relationship of slave owners to their slaves (the letter to Philemon speaks to this); thus, the communities viewed the power relation between master and slave not as a private matter of the owner. It is precisely this practical change that, in its social context, seemed like an attack on the existing "order." H. Thyen suggests a convincing translation for 1 Cor. 7:21. He says one should not try to supplement "if you are able to become free, take advantage of [slavery] (or [of freedom]) all the more"; instead, one should translate with Luther: "If you were able to become free, all the better for you," whereby liberation was only a questionable improvement of one's situation.[2]

The command of 1 Cor. 11:2–6, in which the woman is ordered to submit to the man and which Paul theologically justifies at great length, contradicts the actual equality of women in the churches, where women functioned even as proclaimers of the message (see Rom. 16:1–16). One cannot help but criticize Paul here for lagging behind his own theory (Gal. 3:28) and behind the churches' practice.

The churches make liberation from the power of sin

concrete by their practice of equality and love. Paul has even the distinct hope here that the liberation of the children of God will also bring about the liberation of all creation, even nature (Rom. 8:21). Thus, Paul sees the churches as endowed with a world-changing power, although they may still appear small and insignificant to Roman officials.

The Spirit, Prayer, and Freedom

Every believer receives the Spirit of God (see 1 Cor. 12:13; Acts 2:13, 17). The Spirit of God effects radical change in the entire existence of the believer, who now has escaped the coercive law of sin. Especially chapter 8 in the letter to the Romans clarifies the interdependence of liberation and the Holy Spirit. The Spirit endows people with a new language: that of prayer. They are enabled to express their status as children of God, their status of liberation. Wherever believers, in light of overbearing responsibilities, feel overtaxed, the Spirit takes their place. Thus, in the language of prayer the perfect future of God, the total liberation of all creation, becomes reality even now. Paul has a far-reaching vision: All creation experiences the birth pangs of liberation. Every word of prayer and every Spirit-filled scream is the birth scream of the new creation, a stammering declaration of solidarity with every creature waiting longingly to be set free (Rom. 8:15–27). Many of the Spirit's manifestations within the early Christian communities may appear foreign to us; however, they are, in their sensuousness and physical appearance, fundamental experiences of liberation. The gathered community experiences its newly given power and the joy over its escape in such a dramatic way that—as Luke reports—even the earth trembles (Acts 4:31).

The Spirit of God fills the people with a power enabling them to heal the sick and to speak publicly and uninhibitedly (*parrēsia*). Above all, the situation where believers had to answer for their faith to one tribunal or another had them filled with horror. They feared a lack of words, that they would not know what to say. That was the hour of the Spirit. One was comforted by trusting that the Spirit would speak during that hour (Mark 13:11). Thus, one can understand that even interrogations became a central opportunity of proclamation. These mostly little-educated, yet Bible-knowing people overcame their fear and spoke the truth: that Christ has risen and that there is no longer any other ruler of the world apart from God.

The change through the Spirit also enabled people to experience the gift of joy and happiness. The parable of the lost son (Luke 15:11–32) expresses this side of new existence in an especially clear way. People are bound to each other through the joy that the misery of the lost children has come to an end. The feast of rejoicing actually takes place only when no one is left standing outside. All gifts of the Spirit represent a connection between the child of God and God, but also a connection of the people with each other—and not only those who are members of the faith community. Whoever has experienced the joy of liberation will not rest until seeing the spreading of this freedom wide and far. The believer is permanently in the situation of the father that is described at the end of the parable of the lost son. The father is standing outside and wooing the older son, who does not feel he belongs. The wooing power of early Christianity was immense. Even though believers clearly stated that God would punish the one committing injustices, they still wooed that person with great enthusiasm. Loving one's enemies meant emulating God, ruler over all creation.

One can glean, mainly from the Pauline texts, that the gift of the Spirit also led to an exuberance that, to

Paul, was exaggerated and reckless. Concerning meat sacrificed to idols, some no longer wanted to exercise cultic caution. In the ancient world, almost all meat was butchered in a cultic way. Hence, buying and eating meat meant by necessity the participation in another cult. Paul states that we have, indeed, the freedom to overcome this cultic caution and the fear of touching cultically related things. After all, other cults are without religious significance to us. However, there are people next to us who cannot cope with that, and it is them we have to be mindful of (1 Cor. 10:29). So it still can be necessary to renounce the newly gained opportunities for the sake of others (see also 1 Cor. 9:1, 12, 15).

The Spirit of God in the believers produced equality among humans, for it was one and the same Spirit who was given as one and not in varying quality (see 1 Cor. 12:4–11). It was precisely the attempts of the early Christian communities to make equality among believers a practice that show what obstacles this new life caused in an everyday world. The society of antiquity was organized in hierarchical fashion down to the last fiber of human relationships. Mark reports Jesus as saying, however: "But it shall not be so among you" (Mark 10:43 par., RSV). Still, the plea of the sons of Zebedee shows (Mark 10:37 par.), as does 1 Corinthians 12, that it is not all that easy to practice equality, even in a small church, when the society is built on hierarchic power structures among people. It was not possible to form new concepts and practice different ways at a day's notice. For that reason, the Christians in New Testament times found a completely radical solution to this problem. They said that everybody was to assume the lowest position, which means everybody was to serve, *diakonein*. In antiquity, the word *diakonia* identifies the role of one at the bottom of social hierarchy, that is, the role of slaves or children or women. Equality develops in practice only where power structures among people are ended (Mark 10:42–45 par.; see Rom. 12:16).

The process of liberation occurs whenever those "at the bottom" organize their lives by the power of God's Spirit. The powerful always claim it is they who liberate the powerless, but that kind of "liberation" brings about only bondage because the powerful cannot distinguish between justice and injustice. Only the afflicted—and God, who takes their side—can make such a distinction. Such was the historical experience of early Christianity.

Notes

1. As E. Käsemann has summarized the idea of Rom. 12:1–2 in *Exegetische Versuche und Besinnungen* (Göttingen, 1964), 2:198.

2. See H. Thyen in F. Crüsemann and H. Thyen, *Als Mann und Frau geschaffen* (Gelnhausen, 1978), 158–59.

2

How Justified Is the Feminist Critique of Paul?

Paul's Letters as Sources for the History of Christian Women

Like all biblical traditions, Paul speaks an androcentric language. He mentions women only when there is a special reason; normally, however, they are not mentioned. Thus, he consistently addresses the churches as *adelphoi* (brothers) not because he wants to exclude the thereby addressed women, but because he defines, with self-evident androcentric thinking in a patriarchal society, the churches from the standpoint of their men.[1] The absence of Mary Magdalene and other women from Paul's list of those who have seen the risen one (1 Cor. 15:3–8; cf. Matt. 28:9–10; John 20:14–18; Mark 16:9–11;

implicitly also Mark 16:1–8 par.) could stem from the androcentric language and also from the fact that to Paul or those who passed on his message, women were not all that important.[2]

Despite their androcentric language, Paul's letters are a rich source for the history of Christian women. In his letters, Paul does not turn out to be one to suppress women's history, or at least he suppresses that history much less than his later Christian interpreters, who often found reason to reinterpret Pauline texts in a patriarchal manner. So, to begin with, we shall not report here on the feminist critique of Paul, but on the feminist-historical research freeing Paul from the bonds of reading the Bible in a hierarchic-patriarchal way.

The best-known example for that is Rom. 16:7. Here, Paul speaks—in a greeting list—quite self-evidently of the apostle Junia. Only since the Middle Ages, and primarily because of Luther's translation, has the view prevailed that Junia was not a woman but a man by the name of Junias, although there are no proofs that such a male name existed. This view holds that because the person is called an apostle, that person cannot have been a woman.[3] Although Junia is commonly considered a man even in newer scholarly commentaries on the letter to the Romans, one is here, in the prevailing exegetical work of Germany,[4] most likely to find a reception of feminist-historical work; however, one never sees that the historical significance of women in the spread of the gospel is honored sufficiently.[5]

From Paul's letters, six points become clear: (1) Women had governing functions in the churches. (2) Their energy represented an important contribution to the spread of the gospel. (3) Paul considers women who labor in spreading the gospel equal in rank to himself. (4) He is familiar with submitting to women. (5) To Paul, there is no gender-specific work in the churches. (6) Paul does not see himself at all in the role of the most important apostle and missionary.

In the following, I shall give text examples for these six points. On point (1): The fact that Phoebe is called *prostatis* (Rom. 16:2) means that she had decision-making and leading functions, to which also Paul submitted. The standard translation of the word as "assistant" or "aide" presupposes that the feminine form of the word *must* mean something different than the masculine since the *prostatēs* is the protector, patron, administrator—in any case, a person one submits to.[6] Also the title *diakonos*, which Paul uses in respect to Phoebe, points to Phoebe's leading role, in which she proclaims the gospel and builds churches just like Paul (see 1 Cor. 3:5, 9).[7] It is typical of the history of New Testament exegesis that the word group *diakonein, diakonos* (serving, servant) receives a sexist translation by New Testament scholars the moment the words refer to women. Concerning the service of women, one automatically seems to imagine nursing, special care for women, and matters related to food.[8] One need not summon additional proof of the fact that Prisca is one of the most important people for the work of the gospel at the time, since Paul writes that not only he but "all churches of the Gentiles" owe gratitude to her and her husband (Rom. 16:4). Phoebe, Prisca, and Junia had similarly international roles as evangelists, just as Paul himself did. The list of references to leading functions of women in the letters of Paul could still be expanded.[9]

Concerning point (2), regarding the important work share of women: It may suffice to point to the ratio of men to women in the greeting list of Romans 16, where both male and female laborers for the gospel are mentioned. Next to seventeen men, one finds nine women—an amazing number in the context of patriarchal conditions.

The fact that Paul, without any problem, deems women to be of equal rank to him (point [3]) can be gleaned from his remarks on Prisca, Junia, Phoebe, and also on Euodia and Syntyche in Phil. 4:2–3; furthermore, the above fact is supported by the use of the words *synergos* (co-worker) and *kopian* (to work) in respect to women (Rom.

16:6, 12). The word *kopian*,[10] which is typical for Paul, describes the comparison of his work—and comparable work—with physically hard work and is used by him, full of respect, also in regard to women. It is through Paul, also, that we find out that women ended up in prison and risked their lives for their work, just as he himself and other missionaries had (Rom. 16:4, 7; Phil. 4:3).

As to point (4): Paul did not feel that submitting to women, as in 1 Cor. 16:16, was a problem; else, he would not have formulated, "Submit also to...anyone who works with you [*synergounti*] and works hard [*kopiōnti*]" [trans. from author's German]. From the above findings, one can conclude that the work in the churches was not gender-specific (point [5]).

It should have become apparent that Paul did not see himself as the main bearer of the early Christian mission but as one among many (point [6]). Concerning Junia and Andronicus, for example, Paul mentions respectfully that they had become Christians before him (Rom. 16:7). "Paul and his coworkers" is the title used in exegetical literature to refer to the kind of information concerning all these women and the respective male missionaries.[11] This title produces already a skewed picture. Paul was one among many men and women, and he viewed himself that way—not as the boss of a host of coworkers with unique significance for the gospel.

The above-mentioned matters have been brought to the fore in great clarity only because of the feminist-historical research on Paul by Elisabeth Schüssler Fiorenza and other women and men.[12] One sees thus far no response to these (and other) findings of feminist research on the part of the New Testament scholarship of Catholicism and Protestantism.[13] It is no polemical exaggeration to say that the history of women that one can reconstruct from Paul's letters is either not acknowledged or distorted in New Testament scholarship all the way up to the present. The same applies to the findings of feminist-historical studies since they, too, are neither acknowledged nor discussed. The reason for this, in my view, is that an acknowledgment of the unlimited equality of women would question all institutions of society in a fundamental way. The findings on the above-sketched history of Christian women in the churches of the Roman Empire question the factually present gender hierarchy in the churches as well as the exegesis and the hermeneutical discussion of the Bible bound up with it. New Testament studies, also, are challenged by feminist-historical studies. For that reason it is necessary to talk in the next section—not yet about the feminist critique of Paul—about the feminist critique of existing biblical theological scholarship in the United States and in Western Europe.

On the Feminist-Historical Method

In contemporary biblical scholarship, Paul is researched primarily as a theological thinker of unmatched stature. The connection of his thought with that of life's reality and with the practice of faith in the Christian communities is thereby pushed to the side. The sociologies of early Christianity or even of Christian social ethics are considered marginal concerns, which can be, in any attempt to understand Paul's theology, bracketed without causing any harm. The feminist-historical method, however, questions this form of study that is primarily oriented on the history of thought. Subjects of feminist-historical theology are the reconstruction of the (forgotten) story of Christian women, the critical examination of conventional biblical exegesis, and the development and rediscovery of a *holistic theology*.[14] The point is not to place a female-oriented counterpart next to a one-sided patriarchal theology and its biblical studies, thus making the former a supplement to the latter. Instead, one wants to do the kind of theology that does not continue to legitimize and repeat the socially presupposed hierarchies. A holistic theology is, in this sense, genuinely related to the Jewish and Christian view of God, as will be seen later on in the discussion of Gal. 3:28. A holistic theology means, on the one hand, that all people are equal in this view; hence, the (mostly subconscious) one-sided view of God and humanity from the perspective of white, well-to-do men is no longer perpetuated. On the other hand, a holistic theology means that the interrelationship among Christian thought, action, and the context in which this thought and action takes place is taken seriously.

The implication of this for *hermeneutics* is that exegetes account for *their own context*, both to themselves and to others. I cannot abstract myself from the fact that I live as a well-to-do woman under the particular political and social conditions of Germany; I can, however, try not to exclude other people from my thought and action. This means for the historical method that one has to take into account the *social context of historical documents* and that one has to try to understand theology—such as Paul's—in the context of the social and Christian reality of the churches of his time. The churches are the relevant bearers of the story of early Christianity, not the individual Paul. Such a methodology does not atrophy the importance of Paul's theology; instead, it makes it more concrete.

The historical method of feminist theology is the *social-historical method*.[15] Since this method asks about the history of women in the context of holistic theology, its subject is the history of female and male Jews, female and male slaves, poor and rich women and men, *and* the history of human liberation from the oppression people initiated. As a social-historical method, the feminist-historical method is also a *historical-critical method*. It is a misconception and limitation of the historical-critical method when the latter is practiced in a mere thought-historical fashion and the social questions as posed by feminist theology and social history are ignored. This limitation of the historical-critical method in theology has occurred only since the end of the nineteenth century. The fact that historical-critical exegesis would have to be also social-historical exegesis is, though largely acknowledged, not practiced.[16]

The realization that the hierarchical distinctions between men and women are the outcome of social coercion is closely connected with the realization that distinctions of race and class are injustices before God. Hence, feminist theology is a *liberation theology;* it is liberation theology in the context of women and men in the first world, where it is located primarily. Nevertheless, feminist theology criticizes also liberation-theological views that do not recognize the twofold oppression of women in the so-called third world. At any rate, the connection of women's liberation with comprehensive social justice is maintained by feminist theology.[17]

Since it is a holistic liberation theology, feminist theology is increasingly aware of the *problem of a theological anti-Judaism,* which Christian theology is only just now beginning to overcome. Lack of awareness of this problem has led, mainly in the beginnings of feminist theology, to the tendency to gauge the story of Jesus and the women in Jesus' following against a dark Jewish backdrop hostile to women. Feminist theology has uncritically repeated anti-Jewish clichés of exegetical tradition, so that, for example, S. de Beauvoir considers Paul a woman-hater who continued "the passionately anti-feminist tradition of Judaism."[18] One basis for such misconceptions is the Christian exegetical tradition of juxtaposing Gal. 3:28, for example, and the Jewish morning prayer, where the Jewish man thanks God that God did not make him a Gentile, a slave, or a woman;[19] another basis may be the exegetical tradition in Christian presentation of the situation of the "woman in Judaism."[20] Granted, animosity toward women existed in both Jewish and Christian history—one need think only of 1 Tim. 2:12–15; nevertheless, such an eclectic juxtaposition of antifeminist Jewish remarks and women-friendly Christian remarks is both historically and theologically incorrect. Instead, one needs to see the Jesus movement as an inner-Jewish liberation movement (also of women) that can pick up where previous (including feminist) liberation traditions left off and that tries to overcome patriarchal structures in Judaism and in the Greco-Roman world.[21] With the methodological starting point of feminist-historical research being the people (women and men) who passed on the biblical tradition and their social and Christian reality, a number of basic assumptions of Pauline exegesis will change. The relationship between Paul and the churches is understood differently. The historical situation is depicted as little in the notion of "Paul and his coworkers" as in that of "Paul and *his* churches." Also, the discussion of Pauline texts as a counterstrike against the "opponents" of Paul introduces a structure into the texts they do not have. Paul's debates are much less fundamental than is usually assumed; they also should not be understood as a victory of proper doctrine over extremism and heresy. In such a thought pattern, the women are mostly regarded as emancipation-crazed "womenfolk," who are the "soul of opposition against the apostle and his rigorous discipline."[22] By challenging this exegetical pattern where Paul, as the representative of proper doctrine, is shown in battle with emancipated womenfolk and other heretics, one touches the root of a long tradition of biblical interpretation. Likewise, the biblical interpretation of dominant contemporary exegesis (which handles historical critique in a narrow fashion) defends Paul and expresses itself in the voice of apologetics. Such exegetes defend not only Paul but also their own (male-dominated) institutional church and its theology. E. Schüssler Fiorenza says, "The task of the historian is not the theological justification of Paul but the rediscovery of the life and practice of the early Christian communities."[23]

Paul's Most Important Comments on the Role of Women

Galatians 3:26–28

It is likely that Paul cites a baptismal confession in Gal. 3:26–28; at the least, the decisive sentences of this text express the self-understanding of the Christian churches at the time of Paul, as is also evident by the numerous analogies in Paul's other letters (1 Cor. 7:19; 12:13; Col. 3:11; Gal. 5:6; 6:15). Paul says, "As many of you as were baptized into Christ have clothed yourselves with Christ. There is no longer Jew or Greek, there is no longer slave or free, there is no longer male or female; for all of you are one in Christ Jesus."

On the one hand, the society of the Roman Empire is determined by the deep contrast between low and high, the contrast between the relatively poor population and a small upper class of little more than 1 percent. Besides this vertical separation of society, there exist many horizontal social opposites: that of slaves and free, of those liberated and those free, of women and men, of non-Romans and Roman citizens.[24] From the perspective of many non-Jews, the Jews are a despised people. These horizontal differences with their dependencies and forms of discrimination, though not leveling the vertical gap, play an important role in everyday life. As Paul's letters show, the idea of dissolving the horizontal social differences is closely related with the broadly documented Jewish and Christian tradition of the (eschatological) reversal of high and low social conditions. Paul refers to this reversal in 1 Cor. 1:26–31: "Consider your own call, brothers: not many of you were wise according to the flesh, not many were powerful, not many were of noble birth. But God chose what is foolish in the world to shame the wise" (NRSV alt.). The elevation of the lowly by God's act of electing and calling is the guiding thought in Paul, even concerning the slave question (1 Cor. 7:22). Within the Christian communities, the male and female slaves were to be brothers and sisters to their slave owners both in the Lord *and in the flesh,* as Paul formulates with emphasis (Philemon 16). One could criticize Paul on the slave question only if one were to regard the word "brother" in Philemon 16 as a pious convention that has no corresponding actuality. The founding of churches where slaves and masters are equal is a more permanent overthrow of slavery than a freedom manifesto without steps toward practical application. The community between Jewish Christians and Gentile Christians in the churches is also supposed to include sharing meals at the table, which was to Jewish Christians a problematic point due to Jewish food regulations (see Gal. 2:11ff.). What, then, does Gal. 3:28 say about the relationship between men and women?

According to a broad tradition of interpretation, Gal. 3:28 is meant in an eschatological sense. The ideal would be for the saved to look like angels so that all gender differences were removed; only pneumatological enthusiasts incorrectly view this ideal as an "emancipation pushing for equality." Paul is held to counter this enthusiastic illusion by an eschatological caveat.[25] It is said that Paul and the pre-Pauline traditions—so, another interpretation—argue "strictly *theologically* and do not push for immediate, social change"; social reality may be affected because of the earnest character of what was proclaimed;

still, Gal. 3:28 cannot be considered a social program.[26] In face of such interpretations of the phrase "being in Christ," as in Gal. 3:26–28 (or in any possible pre-Pauline tradition), the ecclesiological interpretation of the phrase is to be stressed since it is usually downgraded in these interpretations. After all, it cannot be refuted that the state of being in Christ is lived in the *church*. And, whenever the ecclesiological meaning of being in Christ is seen, as in Gal. 3:26–28, one will find still another interpretation: In Christ, the social differences are irrelevant; they remained the same and did not change.[27] Nevertheless, all of the above interpretations dislodge the change in gender roles: namely, into the eschaton, into consciousness, or into the camp of enthusiasts; at the same time one assumes that within the Christian practice of the churches and of Paul, gender differences remained as before. And even where such interpretations are rejected, one finds the assumption that "gender-specific differences... cannot be denied for the sake of an abstract ideology of equality." The gender difference is "taken seriously... as a place of grace and obligation."[28] The secular version of this thought would be: "equal, yet different"; hence, the question of who defines being "different" would be eliminated. In Christian history up to now, "being different" has been defined by social, patriarchal power.

There are two relevant feminist arguments against all these interpretations: the history of the female Christians in the churches at the time of Paul and the Jewish and Christian idea of God. One cannot deny that equality of women was practiced in the early Christian communities (see above); neither can one deny that Paul accepted it. The second feminist argument is, in my view, the Jewish and Christian idea of God. A long Jewish tradition exists in which God is the God of the weak, a God who elevates the lowly. "By the hand of a woman," this God has saved the people, as the book of Judith repeatedly reports. The salvation of the entire nation begins at the bottom with the elevation of the lowly. For that reason, Hannah and

Mary are, as women and with their songs about the elevation of the lowly, the hands of this God (Judith 8:33; 9:10; 13:15; 1 Sam. 2:1–10; Luke 1:46–55). Precisely because God is a God of the entire people, of the entire creation, God's actions are partial. Separating this relationship of God into religious and secular realms would fundamentally contradict this view of God. The relationship of God includes all areas of human life, also social reality. The practice of women's equality in the Jesus movement and in the Christian communities at the time of Paul was a result of the Jewish and Christian idea of God and of eschatology. The state by which women and men were in Christ was no longer defined by gender roles and marriage. Galatians 3:28c does not contend "that there are no longer men and women in Christ, but that patriarchal marriage—and sexual relationships between male and female—are no longer constitutive of the new community in Christ."[29] The odd formulation (on account of integrating Gen. 1:27, as it appears in LXX) of no longer "being male and female" is mainly directed at this reality of society's relationship to gender, which is oriented on sexuality, marriage, and procreation. Male and female Christians in their relationship to each other and in their role within the church are no longer defined by patriarchal marriage and sexuality.

The deep distrust of sexuality, which Paul experiences and practices, has its root less in his seeing the social differences between the sexes and more in the ideas of purification and sanctification.

1 Corinthians 7

First Corinthians 7 is Paul's transposition of the baptismal confession of Gal. 3:28 into practical advice for dealing with sexuality. His suggestions are: The best solution is celibacy, as he himself practices. Celibacy, the renunciation of sexual relations, is a charisma (1 Cor. 7:7) and enables one to have an unrestricted relationship with the Lord (7:32), to have an existence as a slave of Christ. Widows, single persons, the engaged, and the divorced should not enter future marriages if possible. Marriage is necessary only when the particular person is not able to practice sexual abstinence. It is good and reasonable within an existing marriage to practice abstinence for a given time after mutual consent, so one can give undivided attention to prayer. Just as the slave in the church is viewed as one liberated by Christ (7:22), Christian husbands should have wives as if they did not have them (7:29). Though they live in a *douleia*, in the slavery of marriage, they do so as those liberated by Christ. Primarily because of viewing marriage from the standpoint of sexuality, Paul regards marriage as enslavement by the partner (see 7:3–4 in the context of 6:12) and as bonding with the power of this world (7:33–34).[30]

One can find such a bedevilment of sexuality even more in antiquity's history of religion and in later church history. The reason for it was certainly not an interest in the liberation of women. On the contrary, the woman appears in this connection as the bearer of this dangerous sexuality (1 Cor. 7:1). Regarding the effects of this view on the churches' practice, however, the sanctified (7:34) virgins and single women—divorced women, for example—may have experienced an equality unusual for antiquity. It seems to have slipped Paul's mind in 1 Cor. 7:29–35 that couples did missionary work right beside and even ahead of Paul; otherwise, he could not have made the sweeping generalization: "The married person [male and female] is concerned with the things of this world" (7:33, 34 [trans. from author's German]).[31]

Overall, Paul thinks that through God's calling even marital slavery is abandoned, just as the slave, due to God's calling, is liberated by Christ. The *klēsis*, the calling, does not have reference to the status quo becoming irrelevant in terms of worldly orders (as 1 Cor. 7:20

is often understood as saying), but to the revolutionary act of God, who chooses the foolish things in this world, turns slaves into free people, liberates from the imprisonment in patriarchal marriage, and makes for a new relationship between marriage partners (7:29).[32] Although the bedevilment of sexuality was not in the interest of women's liberation, Paul's conclusion—the change of the patriarchal marriage and its predominance—actually had liberating effects on women. It is only later in the history of Christianity—when a so-called Christian (actually patriarchal) marriage became associated with the Pauline understanding of sexuality—that one could no longer escape slavery in marriage.

Measured by the social reality in the Roman Empire, three factors concerning the role of women in early Christianity are definitely revolutionary: (1) the dethronement of marriage and family as the state's central pillar of society; instead, the congregation becomes the significant social unit; its goal, however, is not an orderly society but the reign of God; (2) restraint as regards procreation; the passage of Gen. 1:28, "be fruitful and multiply," is not cited; one finds such an admonition only toward the end of New Testament times (1 Tim. 2:15); (3) the changed role of women; after all, equality before God has consequences for a life of togetherness in the church.

1 Corinthians 11:2–16

While from a feminist perspective the passage of 1 Corinthians 7 is still quite ambivalent, 1 Cor. 11:2–16 is no longer so.

In 1 Cor. 11:2–16, Paul wants to implement, through various arguments, a certain attire for women while praying and prophesying. Unfortunately, one can no longer determine with certainty what kind of attire Paul is talking about. One can think that he wants women either to wear a head cover according to conservative moral tradition[33] or to wear their hair tied into a certain hairdo.[34] In this case, then, the women would have an interest in wearing their hair open during worship as an expression of their pneumatological empowering for praying and prophesying, as was common in other cultures of the Greco-Roman world. So, when Paul argues for a head cover, he advocates purely patriarchal power interests; when he opposes wearing the hair open, he advocates, as in the question of speaking in tongues—which is less controversial to feminist theology—a worship that does not appear repulsive to outsiders.

The answer to the difficult question of which custom is meant here, however, is not the only important one for the feminist evaluation of the text. Although one may gravitate toward the more women-friendly interpretation (refusal of open hair in worship), the problem remains of the partially massive argument concerning the (social) difference of the sexes: In verse 3, Paul calls the man the *kephalē*, the head, of the woman. Even when translating the word as "source," which is linguistically possible,[35] the clearly hierarchical order of superiority and inferiority remains in the following sequence: God–Christ–man–woman. The argument regarding the creation story in verses 7–9 points also to ranking the man above the woman. The argument from nature (*physis*) in verse 14, which is certainly an argument of social custom, also strengthens the difference between man and woman: Long hair is an embarrassment to a man and an honor for the woman. In verses 11 and 12, however, Paul formulates two sentences that are supposed to express the equality among the sexes: Both man and woman are mutually dependent on each other when *en kyriō*, in the Lord; or, they are not different—since *chōris* can mean that also.[36] Due to the word *plēn*, meanwhile, at the beginning of verse 11, it is apparent that Paul wants to, in spite of his arguments, maintain the equality of the sexes *en kyriō*, in the Lord, in the sense of Gal. 3:28. In verse 12, however, Paul then factually neutralizes his argument of verse 8. The question of gender equality presents itself as unbalanced here; in fact, it is a matter in which contending tendencies within Paul's thought express themselves. As I see it, one may conclude only that both Paul and the churches in which he lived were still very much in the process of determining this matter.[37]

1 Corinthians 14:33b-36

One frequently considers 1 Cor. 14:33b-36 as a secondary, post-Pauline interpolation.[38] Yet no convincing argument exists to prove this assumption. The passage states that women with Christian husbands are not supposed to talk during worship and ask questions in order to learn. This admonition is connected with the admonition of those speaking in tongues (14:27ff.) and of prophets (14:29ff.), who are supposed to remain quiet if no interpreter is at hand and who are told not to prophecy at the same time. The submission Paul demands here from the wives is a submission to their husbands. Because neither the repression of wives' public speaking during worship service nor the demand of submission is all that far from the basic thought of 1 Cor. 11:2-16, both of those demands will have to be attributed to Paul.

For the same reason, one can conclude that the break—also asserted by traditional exegesis—in Paul's argument of 1 Cor. 11:2-16 cannot be smoothed out. How is it possible that Paul, who lives and works side by side with Prisca and many other women "in the Lord," can formulate sentences such as 1 Cor. 11:3? How can a man who is friends with Christian couples such as Prisca and Aquila formulate a sentence such as 1 Cor. 7:33? How is it possible that a man living with such women as Junia and Prisca and wanting to practice the equality of the sexes in Christ can write such sentences as 1 Cor. 14:33b–36? In all these instances, Paul does not annul equality, yet he limits it in a discriminatory way when it comes to concrete practice. Women are to wear their hair in a certain way while praying or prophesying, or they are to cover it to show order (and subordination); wives of Christian husbands are not to talk in worship and ask questions; instead they should ask their men at home.

All these limitations are to promote the well-being of the church (1 Cor. 14:40; see 7:35); they are to prevent disorder (14:33) and maintain what is customary in the congregation (11:16).

The Feminist Critique of Paul

Elisabeth Schüssler Fiorenza is very generous in her judgment of Paul since she bases her analysis on the concrete situation of the churches' practice and views passages such as 1 Cor. 11:3 not as proclamations about the general annulment of gender equality. She summarizes her critique, however, as follows:

In both passages [1 Cor. 11:2–16 and 14:33b–36], then, Paul places a limit and qualification on the pneumatic participation of women in the worship service of the community. We do not know whether the Corinthian women and men accepted his limitations and qualifications. However, the love patriarchalism of the deutero-Pauline household codes and the injunctions of the Pastorals are further developments of Paul's arguments, developments that will lead in the future to the gradual exclusion of all women from ecclesial office and to the gradual patriarchalization of the whole church.[39]

This critique is justified. The long history of the discrimination and oppression of women in Christianity is dependent on Pauline texts. Feminist-historical research of women leads to differentiated results in evaluating Paul.

Besides this historical-theological research on Paul, there exists within feminist theology another treatment of Paul that is, however, hard to document. I know of this criticism of Paul mainly through oral comments. Many women refuse to deal with Paul at all since his letters have to a great extent determined, and in their opinion originated, the history of the oppression of women in the church. Jesus has a much better feminist reputation than Paul.[40] An exegetical discussion, as I have carried on here, appears to many female critics of Paul as a vain endeavor. I can understand the anger toward Paul and Pauline exegesis, yet I cannot accept it. One can certainly identify Paul with everything women correctly criticize in a male-dominated church, yet one thereby ignores the historical reality of Paul and neglects an important piece of liberation history of Christian women.

Gauged against today's self-understanding of the male church and male theology, Paul was of the feminist avant-garde. He tried to live out Gal. 3:28. One should not be surprised that he was so inconsistent in his efforts. Experiences of liberation are found only at the end of a long path and are accompanied by many setbacks. I wish we were with our church again at the point Paul was: at the point concerning women, the so-called office, the poverty of the poor, and the liberation by Christ.

Notes

1. On the androcentric language of Paul, which is understood by its interpreters either generically (women are included) or as gender-specific (women are not included when a leading position, such as "apostle," is mentioned), see E. Schüssler Fiorenza, *In Memory of Her: A Feminist Theological Reconstruction of Christian Origins* (New York: Crossroad, 1983), 44ff. W. Schrage sees the problem of androcentric language in the New Testament, but he disagrees that by that language the church is defined from the standpoint of men; see E. S. Gerstenberger and W. Schrage, *Frau und Mann* (Stuttgart, 1980), 125. The term "brotherhood," however, must be understood here in the Pauline context in which there was an awareness of equality only among men, not among all people.

2. E. Schüssler Fiorenza assumes that the women are included among the "five hundred brothers" of 1 Cor. 15:6; see her "Die Frauen in den vorpaulinischen und paulinischen Gemeinden," in B. Brooten and N. Greinacher, eds., *Frauen in der Männerkirche* (Munich, 1982), 112–40, 125; English translation, "Women in the Pre-Pauline and Pauline Churches," *USQR* 33 (1978): 153–66, 157. See also Schrage, *Frau,* 131. If one assumes a first appearance of the risen one to Mary Magdalene, one cannot say, as Schrage does (p. 132): "At any rate, there was no basic or sexist resistance in the tradition of the early Christian tradition to women's being witnesses of the resurrection." Why, then, does 1 Cor. 15:3–5 not mention Mary Magdalene? On these questions, see also chap. 8, below.

3. B. Brooten, "Junia... hervorragend unter den Aposteln (Röm. 16,7)," in E. Moltmann-Wendel, ed., *Frauenbefreiung,* 3d ed. (Munich, 1982), 148–51.

4. For example, in W. Schrage, *Frau*, 133; on that passage see U. Wilckens, *Der Brief an die Römer*, EKKNT, 6 (Zurich, 1982), 3; G. Lohfink ("Weibliche Diakone im Neuen Testament," in G. Dautzenberg et al., eds., *Die Frau im Urchristentum* [Freiburg, 1983], 320–38, esp. 327–32) also points clearly to regrettable opposing examples (e.g., Nestle-Aland, *NT Graece*, 26th ed.; *Einheitsübersetzung der Heiligen Schrift* [1979]).

5. Mainly Schrage (*Frau*, 142) tries to do justice to the historical significance of women Christians in New Testament times. But even he has problems (much like Lohfink, "Weibliche," 325) seeing Phoebe as a "woman patron" or a "woman administrator." On Schrage's distinctions between partnership and equality, which could be criticized from a feminist perspective, see below on Gal. 3:28.

6. H. Schaefer, "*Prostatēs*," in PWSup 9, cols. 1301–4. A special meaning of the feminine form of the word is assumed by W. Bauer, *Wörterbuch zum Neuen Testament*, 5th ed. (1958), col. 1425. B. Reicke is a little more circumspect in his article on *proistēmi* in *TWNT* 6:703, 3–4. On the feminist argument, see Schüssler Fiorenza, "Die Frauen," 127 and *In Memory*, 170–72. The Zürcher Bible translates "assistant"; Lohfink (in "Weibliche") translates "helper"; and Schrage (in *Frau*) translates "assistant." The translations need to indicate that they are about females.

7. See on that Schüssler Fiorenza, *In Memory*, 171. Schrage (*Frau*, 141–42) and Lohfink ("Weibliche," 325–26) seem to go the same direction.

8. In light of the exceptions mentioned in the preceding note, one should not overlook the flood of exegetical traditions on this problem. See on that, for example, chap. 8, below; see also the examples in Schüssler Fiorenza, *In Memory*, 170. Both the Pauline idea on the gifts of the Spirit as well as Mark 10:42–45 par. (John 12:26; 13:1–7) show that through Christ *every male and female* Christian is a servant of *all*, and a leading position is not necessarily a hierarchical "office"; see especially E. Käsemann, *Commentary on Romans* (Grand Rapids, Mich.: Wm. B. Eerdmans Publishing Co., 1980), on Rom. 16:2. E. Schweizer, however, insists in the case of Mark (with whom he deals in his context) on the difference between "disciples" and women followers, and on the fact that *diakonia* of women

be table service (see "Scheidungsrecht der jüdischen Frau? Weibliche Jünger Jesu?" *EvT* 42 [1982]: 297–300).

9. See the collection of material in Schüssler Fiorenza, *In Memory*, 160–84.

10. See on that, especially A. von Harnack, *ZNW* 27 (1928): 1–10.

11. For example, W.-H. Ollrog, *Paulus und seine Mitarbeiter* (Neukirchen, 1979).

12. On feminist research concerning Paul, apart from the above-mentioned, see E. Kähler, *Die Frau in den paulinischen Briefen* (Zurich, 1960). The vast American discussion has found hardly any German male or female partners, so far. One needs to point to H. Thyen, "... Nicht mehr männlich und weiblich.... Eine Studie zu Gal. 3,28," in F. Crüsemann and H. Thyen, *Als Mann und Frau geschaffen* (Gelnhausen-Berlin, 1978), 107–201; see also chap. 4, below. Also, see works in the journal *Concilium* and in Brooten and Greinacher, eds., *Frauen*, and Moltmann-Wendel, ed., *Frauenbefreiung*. On the participation of men in this feminist discussion, see H. Pissarek-Hudelist, "Feministische Theologie—Eine Herausforderung?" *ZKT* 103 (1981): 298–308, 400–425, esp. 406ff. However, neither Schrage, *Frau*, nor the authors in G. Dautzenberg et al., eds., *Die Frau*, consider themselves part of a feminist discussion, but rather as part of antifeminist apologetics.

13. See, for example, G. Dautzenberg, "Zur Stellung der Frauen in den paulinischen Gemeinden," in G. Dautzenberg et al., eds., *Die Frau*, 182–224; even though Schüssler Fiorenza's essay "Women" is noted, no discussion with her or another feminist view of the "position of women in the Pauline churches" takes place.

14. On this catchword, see C. Halkes, *Gott hat nicht nur starke Söhne* (Gütersloh, 1980), 43ff.; Pissarek-Hudelist, "Feministische Theologie," 407.

15. This contention relates to the scholarly historical treatment of sources written from a feminist perspective. It is not quite correct to say what M. Monheim-Geffert and R. Rieger state in summarizing the problem of method: "An independent scholarly method within feminist exegetical studies has been developed only in part. Feminist female theologians work from either a feminist-historical-critical, a feminist-sociological, or a feminist-materialistic perspective, depending on the re-

spective theological and political orientation" ("Feministische Bibelauslegung im Kontext der Feministischen Theologie," *BK* [1984]: 4, 142–48, 148). The starting point of the historical-critical method is either social-historical or materialistic, which means it considers the social context of texts. In Germany this method is used in a purely thought-historical manner, and that makes it narrow.

16. H. Conzelmann and A. Lindemann are correct in their vastly used workbook on the New Testament when saying, "The sociological task of form history is, therefore, the question after the *Sitz im Leben*" (*Arbeitsbuch zum Neuen Testament* [Tübingen, 1979], 72). (Then, however, only principles of style and literary forms are discussed under the topic *Formgeschichte*.) In methodological theory and practice, hence, one should not discuss social-historical exegesis as such but the liberation-theological direction of social-historical work vis-à-vis a patriarchal and status-quo-oriented social history.

17. See, e.g., C. Halkes and E. Schüssler Fiorenza.

18. S. de Beauvoir, *Das andere Geschlecht* (1968), 100; English, *The Second Sex* (1953).

19. For a collection of material on this contrast, see H. Paulsen, "Einheit und Freiheit der Söhne [sic] Gottes," *ZNW* 71 (1980): 74–95, esp. 85 nn. 59–61.

20. An example with consequences is A. Oepke's article "Gynē" in *TWNT* 1:781ff. This tradition is massively continued in the (nonfeminist) book by H. Wolff, *Jesus der Mann* (Stuttgart, 1977), 75ff.

21. On these problems, see especially Schüssler Fiorenza, *In Memory*, 195ff.; B. Brooten, "Jüdinnen zur Zeit Jesu," in Brooten and Greinacher, eds., *Frauen*, 141–48.

22. E. von Dobschütz, *Die urchristlichen Gemeinden* (Leipzig, 1902), 34–35. It is the leading doctrine up to this day that 1 Cor. 11:2–16 deals with exaggerated emancipation of Corinthian women; see note 25, below, for further discussion.

23. Schüssler Fiorenza, *In Memory*, 10.

24. For an overview of the social situation of the time, see G. Alföldy, *Römische Sozialgeschichte* (Wiesbaden, 1975).

25. E. Käsemann, "Zum Thema der urchristlichen Apokalyptik," in *Exegetische Versuche und Besinnungen* (Göttingen, 1964), 2:105–31, 125–31. He says, "Christian existence has the reality of childhood only in the freedom of the afflicted, which

points ahead to the resurrection of the dead as the truth and perfection of the *regnum Christi*" (p. 130). Käsemann insists on the physical aspect of Christian existence under Christ's rule. How, then, can he say that the patriarchal order of slavery, of the submission of women, and of the obedience toward the political powers is continually maintained by Paul? (See, E. Käsemann, "Grundätzliches zur Interpretation von Römer 13," in *Exegetische*, 2:204–22, esp. 215–16.) He defends Paul with the women's, slaves', and churches' enthusiasm. How is emancipation to manage withdrawing from everyday life and from serving God (ibid., 218)? Just because I basically agree with Käsemann's interpretation of Paul, I see it necessary to search both Paul and the churches in order to discover the practical and bodily consequences of the everyday worship of women and slaves.

26. Paulsen, "Einheit," 88, 94. He correctly refers to E. Käsemann and not all too correctly to K. Stendahl, *The Bible and the Role of Women* (Philadelphia: Fortress Press, 1975); see also K. Stendahl, "Die biblische Auffassung von Mann und Frau," in Moltmann-Wendel, ed., *Frauenbefreiung*, 118–32. After all, Paul lags, in Stendahl's view, behind the statements made in Gal. 3:28, and now the task is to also realize this equality of the sexes in the church. The repeated assurance that Gal. 3:28 not be a social program (Paulsen, "Einheit," 88, 94, 95) does not do justice to the early Christian and Pauline ecclesiology and its practice in life. There, though not dealing with the program of a new society, the point is a *new life* in the body of Christ.

27. R. Bultmann, *Theologie des Neuen Testaments* (Tübingen, 1954), 305, sec. 34.2; English trans., *Theology of the New Testament* (New York: Macmillan Co., 1955). The fact that worldly distinctions are of no import *en Christō* (in Christ) signals a freedom from the world that allows one to participate in the world at a distance, namely that of *hōs mē* (as if not) (1 Cor. 7:29ff.) (see ibid., 347ff., sec. 40.2).

28. Schrage, *Frau*, 122; his basic thought is: Equality has to be rejected; partnership is the correct way (see also notes 1 and 5, above). Yet, fair partnership is based on equality.

29. Schüssler Fiorenza, *In Memory*, 211.

30. In contemporary exegesis, 1 Cor. 7:3–4 is viewed as if Paul were making positive statements concerning marriage; constant reference is made here to the partnership language.

The verb describing the sexual relation between the sexes is, however, the same as in 1 Cor. 6:12: *exousiazein* (having power over someone), which to Paul means bondage, enslavement by people. There definitely is no valid argument for wanting to fill the verb in 6:12 with a negative connotation ("not letting anything gain power over me") and the verb in 7:3–4 with a positive connotation ("not to rule over one another but mutually to serve one another even in marital questions"), as W. Foerster (*TWNT* 2:571ff.) paraphrases 7:3. "You were bought in cash" by Christ (1 Cor. 6:20; 7:23) means that you are slaves of Christ and are those set free by Christ (7:21); therefore, Christians do not become slaves of people. Paul regards marriage mainly as a problem of sexuality—and sexuality to him is slavery. For that reason, he speaks of circumcision and slavery in 7:17–24 as an *analogy for marriage*.

31. Schüssler Fiorenza, *In Memory*, 173, 231.

32. Exegetical tradition translates the word *klēsis* in 1 Cor. 7:20 mostly—in contrast to the usual meaning of the word—as "state," so that one would have to translate "all are to remain in the state in which they were called" (thus Bauer, *Wörterbuch*, col. 862). There is no convincing linguistic and theological argument for such a translation. See K. L. Schmidt, in *TWNT* 3:492ff.; S. Bartchy, *First-Century Slavery and 1 Corinthians 7:21*, SBLDS, 11 (Missoula, Mont.: Scholars Press, 1973), 134ff. One has to translate, instead, "All should remain in the vocation to which they were called."

33. See chap. 4, below, with a discussion of the religion-historical and cultural-historical materials.

34. Schüssler Fiorenza, *In Memory*, 227–30.

35. For exegetical detail, see chap. 4, below.

36. J. Kürzinger, "Frau und Mann nach 1 Kor. 11,11f.," *BZ* 22 (1978): 270–75.

37. One notes frequently the break in the Pauline chain of arguments in 1 Cor. 11:2–16 and basically with it Paul's contradicting himself on the problem of the women's role; see, for example, Schrage, *Frau*, 98ff.

38. For the older discussion, see Kähler, *Die Frau*, 70–83; for the newer discussion, see Schüssler Fiorenza, *In Memory*, 230–33.

39. Schüssler Fiorenza, *In Memory*, 233.

40. It may be more appropriate to assume a continuity between Jesus and Paul on this question; see on that especially W. Klassen, "Musonius Rufus, Jesus, and Paul: Three First-Century Feminists," in P. Richardson and J. C. Hurd, eds., *From Jesus to Paul: Studies in Honour of Francis Wright Beare* (Waterloo, Ont.: Wilfrid Laurier University Press, 1984), 185–206.

3

"Leaders of the Faith" or "Just Some Pious Womenfolk"?

> Anti-Judaism in German
> New Testament Scholarship

Christian anti-Judaism has expressed itself in both New Testament scholarship and Christian theology by the fact, among others, that Jesus' behavior in dealing with women was portrayed as revolutionary in contrast to the patriarchy of Judaism. Thereby, individual rabbinic sayings were negatively contrasted with stories of Jesus—notably by Christian theologians who, at the same time, did not emulate this ever so women-friendly Jesus, as will be seen from the following material. Although a continuation of this anti-Judaistic tradition still exists (even in feminist theology), all the main points on this question in both methodological and content-related aspects have already been summarized a long time ago as, for example, in Bernadette Brooten's brief 1982 essay.[1] At any rate, it should be possible to describe the history of women in early Christianity and its contemporary Judaism without using anti-Judaistic disqualifications.

With this essay, I should like to highlight the fact that Jewish religion was sustained also by women *groups* and that, on account of this, Christian proclamation was directed to some of these women groups—with partial success. The sources revealing this fact are common knowledge; nevertheless, a recognition of this aspect of women's history is still in the waiting. The respective sources are Josephus (*BJ* 2.560ff.; *Ant.* 20.34ff. [20.2.3]), Martial (*Epigrams* 4.4.7), Juvenal (Satire 6.542ff.), and Acts 13:50; 16:13ff.; 17:4, 12. One still would have to seek out inscription material,[2] and so I will call attention to a task to be continued and do so in the requisite tentative manner.

Since my theological work is done in the context of Germany, my first theological task is to examine and critique Christian anti-Judaism also in this respect. How do Christian authors deal with the historical phenomenon that non-Jewish women subscribed to Judaism when, supposedly, it was quite antiwomen?

One solution, offered by Christians, is that, for propaganda reasons, Jews treated women better than they wanted to in the Diaspora. In his article "Gynē" in the still influential *Theologisches Wörterbuch zum Neuen Testament* (*Theological Dictionary of the New Testament*), A. Oepke begins by saying—in line with the Jesus-versus-Rabbis pattern already referred to—that "to fulfill His calling in relation to women [Jesus] can break rigid Jewish custom with matter-of-fact boldness. Thus, He does not hesitate to speak with a woman."[3]

But then Oepke notices the historical connection between women turning to Christianity and women turning to Judaism, and he explains it as follows: "In the early community there was no doubt as to the full membership of women (Ac. 1:14; 12:12). After the Jewish pattern, but without succumbing to the feminism of Jewish and Gnostic propaganda (Ac. 13:50; 17:4, 12; 2 Tim. 3:6; *Ac. Pl. et Thecl.* 41), the Christian mission wins women from the very outset (Ac. 16:13f.; 17:4, 12, 34; 18:18)."[4]

Although the volume containing Oepke's article appeared in 1933, Oepke's writing is not a particularly national socialist piece but, rather, one typical of Christian anti-Judaism, which is embedded in theological history before 1933 and since 1945. Klaus Thraede is still part of this scholarly tradition when he says: "The reticence [regarding women] within the cult may have also existed in the Diaspora; here, however, the Jewish mission was forced, particularly in the large cities, to take cognizance of the fact that during early imperial times the number of women among those who 'feared God' was growing and to put to rest traditional discriminations."[5] Regarding women, then, the Judaism of the Diaspora would have been some sort of patriarchal wolf in feminist sheep's clothing.

Another explanation for the fact that non-Jewish women joined the Jewish religion can be found in the scholarly commentaries on Acts.[6] It has escaped these authors' attention that Judaism is supposed to be antiwomen, and now either they comment on historical findings in a tone that shows contempt for women or contempt for women's religion in general, or they do not comment at all. Hans Conzelmann (1963) writes laconically on Acts 13:50: "The typical picture. Judaism and women: Josephus, *Bell. jud.*, II, 560"—as if the scholarly tradition did not exist that insists Judaism be antiwomen. Such is also the implicit presupposition of other commentators who express their contempt for women in imaginative assumptions. Jürgen Roloff (1981) writes on Acts 13:50: "Mainly older ladies from distinguished families have a lively interest in Jewish religion.... It may not have been all too difficult to bring them to the point of influencing their husbands and sons, the leading city officials." The New Testament text that is exegeted here says: "Jews, however, implored the God-fearing, respected women and the first of the city and [these?] instigated a persecution against Paul and Barnabas and drove them out of their district" [trans. from author's German]. The text says neither that the women were wives or mothers of city officials nor that the women were easily influenced. The text tells that non-Jewish women with an interest in Judaism formed a separate group, influential in city politics, *apart* from the city's "first."

In a historically relevant part of manuscript tradition, one can even distinguish between two women groups in Acts 13:50: the God-fearing women and the women of prominence. This way of reading deserves preference since it is the more difficult one; the reading "the God-fearing, respected women" could be an attempt at blending with and adapting to Acts 17:4, 12. In Acts, not only women from the upper class are members of Judaism, as is often suggested, but also women groups from the lower classes, as will be shown in the discussion of Acts 16:13. According to the older way of reading, Acts 13:50 could, thus, describe participation in Judaism by women from both the upper class and the lower classes.

Yet even if one assumes that the text version "the God-fearing, respected women" is the older tradition, one does not gain the idea of older, easily influenced, distinguished women who, in turn, influence their husbands and sons (*cherchez la femme*); rather one gains the idea of an independent group of non-Jewish women who are active in city politics and who worship the God of Israel. The compilation of women-despising assumptions in the cited commentary by J. Roloff is not the only one. In commenting on this text, H. J. Holtzmann (1901), for example, says that the women are the "wives of Gentile men," and Erwin Preuschen (1912) assumes the dealings to be "intrigues."

Scholarly commentators have been particularly challenged by the fact that the group of women in Philippi (Acts 16:13–14) gathered in a *proseuchē*, a place of prayer, a synagogue. It is their assumption that it could not have been a synagogue, or the women prayed simply in front of the synagogue in open air. One will have to point here to Bernadette Brooten's work; she shows that it could have very well been a synagogue and that this entire discussion only arose because commentators could not imagine women conducting a worship service on their own.[7] Occasionally, one sees from the commentaries on Acts 16:13–14 that it is suspect to the commentators to have women appear in a synagogue all by themselves since, thereby, these commentators perceive a threat to their *Christian* church. Alfred Wikenhauser (1961) says: "Most likely, men were not entirely absent. Still, a proper Jewish worship service has apparently not taken place." The text, however, tells of a gathering of women without men, attended then by Paul and Silas: "On the Sabbath day we left the city through the gate and went to the river, where we assumed to find a place of worship; and having sat down, we talked to the gathered women" [trans. from author's German]. A. Wikenhauser misinterprets the text though knowing better; after all, he himself had concluded in a different context that in Acts 13:50; 16:13; 17:4, "the women's behavior was mentioned in contrast to the men's."[8] Also, the group in Philippi is a group of non-Jewish women that prays to the God of Israel without men being present. What the text does not say is that their worship is not fully valid. It is as if Christian commentators saw the Christian church through and behind the situation in Philippi. Though H. J. Holtzmann (1901) supposes a gathering in a synagogue, he insists that the gathering not be a worship. He says, "One always finds here, as in Catholic churches, a number of pious womenfolk." He implies, it would appear, that the true worship, the fully valid kind of religion, takes place only when men take charge of the situation. The contempt for women, discussed in a different context as a problem of Judaism, is in reality Christianity's own contempt for women. Sources are reinterpreted simply because they do not fit one's own Christian idea of women.

The fact that groups of upper-class women in Thessalonica and Berea (Acts 17:4, 12) gain proper significance in Jewish religion, and later in the spread of the Christian message, is viewed by Christian commentators only from one aspect, namely that the women belong to the upper class—not that they are women or that they form their own group. The writers of Christian social history are so interested in searching for members of the upper class in early Christianity that they lose sight of members of the lower classes. The women in Thessalonica and Berea are part of those cities' upper class, yet the group of women in Philippi (possibly also some members of the group in Pisidian Antioch, see 13:14) come from the lower classes. Lydia is one of that latter group (Acts 16:14). She earns a living as a seller of purple fabrics—in a profession that is very strenuous and despised due to the bad smell connected with dyeing fabrics purple.[9] The fact that the place of worship is outside the city gates near the river is more likely connected with the usual location of purple-dyeing businesses outside the city than with Jewish ritual.[10] In the textile-dyeing industry in general as in textile industry outside the home, mainly women are employed.[11] The fact that Paul and Silas suspect to find a place of worship near the river means that earlier they had often found women textile workers who were worshiping the God of Israel together.

Overall, we will have to place the contempt for women among the Christian commentators of Acts 13:50; 16:13–14; 17:4, 12 in the context of their contempt for women's religion and for Judaism as a women's religion. Emil

Schürer says about the women worshiping the God of Israel: "Also in this case, as in the case of any religious movement, the hearts of women proved to be the most receptive."[12] Anti-Judaism, contempt for women, and contempt for religion are often closely related. One finds proof for that from the earliest times of Christianity. Juvenal, the satirist, is an excellent representative of this mixture of anti-Judaism, contempt for women, and enlightened contempt for pious people. He says:

> No sooner has that fellow [the official of an Egyptian cult] departed than a palsied Jewess, leaving her basket and her truss of hay, comes begging to her secret ear [a rich Roman woman]; she is an interpreter of the laws of Jerusalem, a high priestess of the tree, a trusty go-between of highest heaven. She, too, fills her palm, but more sparingly, for a Jew will tell you dreams of any kind you please for the minutest of coins.[13]

I cannot discuss in detail here how these sentences can be used in the reconstruction of women's history; nevertheless, one can glean from them, in this context, not only the contempt for Jews, women, and religion, but also that Jewish women were propagating their religion also among women as independent teachers of the law. This text, too, leads one to conclude that Jewish women were entitled to total religious practice even without the presence of men.

The contempt for women, Jews, and religion is also expressed in an epigram by Martial (4.4, 7), where he enumerates repulsive odors, among them the repulsive breath of women fasting on the Sabbath. It must suffice here to call attention to the discussion as to whether there is a false understanding here, given that the Sabbath is not a day of fasting.[14] Since Martial mentions women here especially in connection with Jewish religion, this points again—at least in the context of other literary sources, cited earlier—to women groups practicing the Jewish faith.

In conclusion, one may say concerning scholars' comments on Acts 13:50; 16:13–14; and 17:4, 12 that the implicit or explicit assumption of all these comments is that *"proper" worship is Christian worship only when led by men* (or "proper" religion is Christian religion whose practice is led by men). According to the cited sources, the "feminism" of Jewish propaganda (see the quote by Oepke, above) continued in Christianity, even if Christian commentators cannot grasp this side of New Testament sources.

Women Groups as Bearers of Judaism and Christianity in the First Century

The foregoing discussion of the Christian scholarly tradition on Acts 13:50; 16:13–14; and 17:4, 12 has shown that women groups in the first century played an important role in the spread of Judaism and Christianity, and that the women had also leading and teaching functions. When the Christian Lydia oversees the house church in Philippi, she continues a leading function she already had in the group of women proselytes and sympathizers of Jewish religion. And she does not have to give up this leadership position when Christian men join the house church.

Two texts by Josephus deepen this picture. They show, further, that not only individual women convert to Judaism[15] but also groups of women whose mutuality existed already on other levels, yet then apparently received a new quality from Jewish religion.

This factor is especially true for the upper-class women of Thessalonica[16] and Berea, possibly also for the women in Pisidian Antioch (see above). The fact that these groups of women come under the influence of the missionary activities of Christian itinerant evangelists troubles the leaders of the respective synagogue communities, who, in defense, employ political strategies (Acts 17:1–15). It is clear that these women are of great significance to Jewish communities (see Acts 13:50). The upper classes of the cities in the Roman provinces are used by Rome as an extended arm of central power. Aelius Aristides writes: "There is no need for an occupation force living in fortresses; for the most respected and powerful men everywhere control, in your [Rome's] interest, their own city."[17] When women from this upper class confess the God of Israel (or, in addition, claim Jesus to be the Messiah), they act politically "unwise," measured by the interest of their own class and that of their men. Still, the cities' upper-class men do not appear in Acts 13:50 and 17:8 as sympathizers of Jewish religion, but as safeguards of political order in the interest of Rome. In this context, the situation in Berea (Acts 17:12) is remarkable. The women of the upper class are mentioned as the new Christian believers first, and men later. It is not remarkable here that women are mentioned in the first place[18] but that upper-class men are won over at all. One can only point here to the tragic situation that Jews and Christians of the time fought with each other although both groups, after all, suffered equally under the oppression of the Roman world power.[19]

The two texts from Josephus, which have to be discussed now, relate to another political and cultural situation of the same time period: that of Charax Spasinu and Damascus.

The conversion story of the royal house in Adiabene (Josephus, *Ant.* 20.34ff.) contains a note concerning the "women of the king" in Charax Spasinu, by the Persian Gulf. A Jewish merchant, Ananias, enters the women's chambers of the palace and teaches the women to worship God in the traditional paternal way (*patrion*) of the Jews. By way of these women, the Jewish merchant becomes known to Izates, who is won over in the same way. Izates is a prince from Adiabene and lives in exile in Charax Spasinu. Circumcision does not play a role in this story, although one finds out later that Izates feels circumcision need be a part of his conversion and is surprised to see the Jewish merchant Ananias assume the pragmatic viewpoint of the king's mother, Helena. Then an argument over circumcision ensues between Helena, who had become Jewish in Adiabene independently from her son, and her son. Helena argues politically whereas Izates turns to his Jewish teacher as final arbiter, whereby one can conclude that Izates expects Ananias to require circumcision. Hence, one can conclude that at first, Ananias taught circumcision in Charax Spasinu as self-evident for men, yet did not demand it as something immediately necessary; later on, he sees enough leeway for Helena's political pragmatism on the question. Eventually, another Jewish teacher convinces Izates that circumcision is stringent. The question of circumcision in the connection of a women group's conversion is discussed in such detail since Christian polemics against Jews repeatedly establish a connection between circumcision and the situation of women in Judaism. Many have argued both that women were religiously declassed since only men could be circumcised[20] and that it was easier for women to become Jews since they did not have to take the hurdle of circumcision.[21] The arguments contradict each other and have, as far as I know, no basis in Jewish sources.

At any rate, the story from Charax Spasinu presupposes that women did not perceive male circumcision as implying a declassification of women. Indeed, Izates even comes to the conclusion that only circumcision would help him experience the joy of Jewish religion that his mother had (*Ant.* 20.38). Also, the text does not say that women's conversion is somehow due to the fact that women can become Jews easier than men. Instead, the parallelism between female religious practice and male religious practice, which includes circumcision, is already presupposed.

The king's women in Charax Spasinu became Jews together and were immediately instrumental in winning over other people by making their teacher available to others. Also in this case, the group of women existed already before their conversion, so that the conversion does not create this community. Still, Jewish religion has to have offered a possibility to express the identity of women as a group, an identity that did not exist before. The conversion had to be attractive to this group in the palace as a *group* of women. The men of the palace have no part in this happening. During the conversion of Helena (the king's mother in Adiabene), likewise, no man of the palace is present (*Ant.* 20.35).

One can find out more about the situation of the "king's women" from the book of Esther. The book distinguishes between two houses of women in the palace (Esth. 2:3 and 2:14). In one house reside the beautiful virgins of the country, who are introduced to the king one by one. After the king has spent the night with them, they are taken to the second house and become the king's concubines. Eventually, after the king has chosen one of them to be queen, the remaining virgins are also taken to the second house of women.[22] Then, the concubines are allowed to see the king only when he explicitly calls them. Both houses of women are overseen by a royal officer. The queen does not live in either house but in the king's palace (Esth. 1:9; 4:13).

Presumably, the king's women in Charax Spasinu are the concubines (*pilageshim* in Esth. 2:14) who had hardly any contact with the actual king's palace. It is possible that they addressed the foreign prince Izates through his wife, Princess Samacho (*Ant.* 20.23). Since Josephus is a power-oriented historian, we find out little about the king's women who reside in the house of women.

Josephus mentions them only to explain how the Jewish merchant managed to approach Izates. Since the king's women, as his possessions, are completely subject to him, conversion to a religion other than the king's would already constitute an act of disobedience, unless the king or his official, the women's overseer, approved this new religion. Since Ananias had access to the house of women, one can assume that at least the overseer had approved of the merchant's presence. Yet even if the conversion is not an act of open rebellion, it is still an act of independence that offers the women an orientation other than keeping themselves cosmetically "spiced-up"[23] for the king or having to wait for him for years under presumably hard work as if "ordered and never picked up." The king's mother, Helena of Adiabene, a power-conscious and powerful woman, has taken the same step and become Jewish; yet political reasons may have been at least partially responsible for this step. Her social situation cannot be compared, either, to that of the women in the harem.

It must have been possible for the women of the harem in Charax Spasinu to practice their Jewish faith without the presence of their Jewish teacher and once he had left. Hence, a pure Jewish women's community must have been possible. One can hardly assume that these women viewed themselves as not able to practice fully valid worship. Josephus's note formulates Ananias's message as if the women took on the full Jewish faith and not merely a restrictive substitute. They worship God in "the paternal tradition of the Jews" (*Ant.* 20.34). Hence, the women in the harem had to function on their own as readers and interpreters of the Torah, as leaders of the community of faith, and so on.

Groups of women practicing the Jewish religion existed also in Damascus when the Jewish-Roman War broke out in 66 C.E. (Josephus, *BJ* 2.560ff.). As in many Syrian cities, the Jewish population of Damascus was incarcerated (see 2.461–62). Hatred and fear of Jews

(2.478) played a role here, as well as fear of the Romans (2.461). The incarcerated Jews were murdered somewhat later than in the other Syrian cities—that is, only after the temporary Roman defeat in Judea (2.559). In light of the defeat of the Syrian legate Cestius in Judea, the non-Jewish residents of Damascus probably saw the political necessity to act clearly pro-Rome and to demonstrate their loyalty by murdering the Jews. The only problem was, however, that their own women were practicing Jews. Josephus says, "They distrusted their own wives, however, who, with few exceptions, were attached to the Jewish religion; and their main endeavor, therefore, was to keep them in ignorance of their designs" (2.560). In Damascus, as in other Syrian cities, Jews won over non-Jews for the Jewish faith (see 2.463). These "Judaizing" people were a burden regarding the loyalty toward Rome (2.463). Given that, one might apply to the women of Damascus the following sentence formulated by Josephus (2.463): "Though one did not want, without further ado, to kill the group doubtful in either way [*ioudaizontes*, the Judaizers], one feared them due to their connection with the Jews, as if they were true enemies." The Judaizing women in Damascus are caught in the middle in the same way: They are connected to the Jews and, at the same time, to their non-Jewish men. The men fear to be impeded by the women in their killing of the Jews and, thus, murder the Jews without their women's knowledge. In the eyes of the Romans, however, the situation in Damascus still appeared unreliable in spite of the Jewish pogrom. One has to ask whether the Judaizing women in Damascus were members of the upper class[24] or whether they were women from the entire non-Jewish city population. The politically active group might, indeed, be found in the upper class in light of the pursued Roman interests in this context. Nevertheless, such Jewish pogroms were initiated not only by members of the upper class but also by the rest of the entire population. Hence, one cannot solve the question.

"Leaders of the Faith"

We must incorporate the picture, gained so far, of women groups accepting the Jewish religion or, in connection with it, the Christian faith, into the history of religion—and of women—during the Roman Empire.

Strabo, a writer during the times of Augustus, says:

> All people think that the women are the leaders of the faith [*archēgoi tēs deisidaimonias*]; and it is the women, likewise, who cause the men to become more interested in the cults of the gods, in the feasts, and in the invocations of goddesses [*potniasmos*], and it is rare to find a man at such events who lives by himself. (Strabo, 7.297)

Mainly the Oriental religions are women religions in the eyes of Roman writers and of the leading men of the state. Nevertheless, Strabo's judgment, which he claims is shared by everyone, cannot be applied to the religions supported and enacted by the Roman government, not even to the women cults propagated by the state, which were to "preserve the ideals of female morality."[25] Moreover, one has to presuppose two kinds of religions in the Roman Empire, basically to be distinguished from each other: those intended to support the state's interests of order, class society, and the submission of women; and those gaining solid support although the state considered them a nuisance. The most important independent cults of the time were the Isis cult and Judaism. The persecution of these two religions, for example in the city of Rome, was clearly related to their attraction for Roman women.[26] Already from the connection between the state's politics on women and the persecution of the Isis cult and of Judaism, one can see that both the Isis cult and Judaism gave women opportunities not offered to them by the cults of the state. Susan B. Pomeroy says: "The Roman state religion... traditionally excluded slaves, former slaves, and—with the exception of a few, such as the six vestalic virgins and the two Ceres priestesses—women from their hierarchy of offices, and it separated the religion's participants according to strictly severed categories."[27] The Oriental religions, which the state feared, gave women a higher standing in comparison to the subordinating roles they had in state religion, and they allowed women to participate in leadership functions.[28] The quotation by Strabo points to this fact. Strabo calls the women *archēgoi tēs deisidaimonias* and depicts their general function as initiators[29] who win the men for the cult and their particular function as leaders in bringing about increased cult participation.[30] Strabo's comment corroborates Bernadette Brooten's thesis that the title *archēgissa/archēgos,* found in two Jewish inscriptions, describes the function of leadership of women in the synagogue, perhaps also their function as foundresses of Jewish communities of faith.[31] According to Strabo, both of these functions are conceivable as activities of women.

Both the Isis cult and Judaism (and with the latter, also Christianity) offered women opportunities, greater than those of state-approved religions, for religious culture of their own and for the experience of greater justice in their relationships with the other gender and other classes. The fact that not only single women but entire groups of women thus became "leaders of the faith" had an explosive force in the entire power structure of the Roman Empire. Later critics of Christianity have expressed this point clearly: "These are people who draw on the lowest layers of the population and bring together ignoramuses and credulous womenfolk, who, after all, are easily won over due to the weakness of their gender and form a despicable gang of conspirators" (Minucius Felix, *Octavius* 8.4). Yet it could not be foreseen at this point that Christians themselves would quite soon—at least in the form of their authorized representatives—be standing on the other side, on that of patriarchalism, and would practice contempt for women and Jews.

Notes

1. B. Brooten, "Jüdinnen zur Zeit Jesu," in B. Brooten and N. Greinacher, eds., *Frauen in der Männerkirche* (Munich, 1982), 141–48. See also on this point, E. Schüssler Fiorenza, *In Memory of Her: A Feminist Theological Reconstruction of Christian Origins* (New York: Crossroad, 1983), esp. 105–51.

2. Some inscription material on women groups of other cultures has been collected by R. MacMullen, "Women in Public in the Roman Empire," *Historia* 29 (1980): 208–18.

3. A. Oepke, "Gynē," in *TWNT* (1933), 1:784, 40ff. For the respective rabbinic sentences, see the same, 1:782, 1ff.

4. Oepke, "Gynē," 1:785, 20–25.

5. K. Thraede, "Ärger mit der Freiheit: Die Bedeutung von Frauen in Theorie und Praxis der alten Kirche," in G. Scharffenorth and K. Thraede, *Freunde in Christus werden*... (Gelnhausen, 1977), 92. K. Thraede, "Frau," *RAC* 8 (1972): 227ff., mentions here "assimilation." One finds the same position, for example, in A. Weiser, "Die Rolle der Frau in der urchristlichen Mission," in G. Dautzenberg et al., eds., *Die Frau im Urchristentum* (Freiburg, 1983), 158–81, 165–66.

6. Since these commentaries are easily accessible in every theological library, I will cite in the following only the author's name, year, and Bible passage. In this context, I would also like to call attention to the fact that these scholarly commentaries occupy a place of great power in the reality of the church and that hardly a single one of them exists that was written by a woman. Biblical interpretations by women are not to be found at the center of power.

7. B. Brooten, *Women Leaders in the Ancient Synagogue* (Chico, Calif.: Scholars Press, 1982), 139–40.

8. A. Wikenhauser, *Die Apostelgeschichte und ihr Geschichtswert* (Münster, 1921), 121 n. 4.

9. See chap. 5, below.

10. On the discussion of synagogues by the water, see S. Krauss, *Synagogale Altertümer* (Vienna, 1922), 281–86.

11. N. Kampen, *Roman Working Women in Ostia* (Berlin, 1981), 133.

12. E. Schürer, *Geschichte des jüdischen Volkes im Zeitalter Jesu Christi* (Leipzig, 1908): 3:168.

13. Juvenal, Satire 6.542ff., translation by G. G. Ramsay, Loeb Classical Library. On this Juvenal passage, see also M. Stern, *Greek and Latin Authors on Jews and Judaism* (Jerusalem, 1980), 2:100–101.

14. See Stern, *Greek and Latin Authors*, 1:524.

15. Material collection in Brooten, *Women Leaders*, 144–47; see also K. G. Kuhn and H. Stegemann, "Proselyten," in PWSup 9 (1962): 1263–67.

16. The verse in Acts 17:4 does not say explicitly that these women were proselytes and sympathizers of Jewish religion; however, this fact follows from the parallelism to the previously mentioned group of God-fearing people and from the parallel on the subject in Acts 13:50; 17:12.

17. Aelius Aristides, *Orationes* 26.64; see on that L. Schottroff, "Nicht viele Mächtige: Annäherungen an eine Soziologie des Urchristentums," in *Befreiungserfahrungen: Studien zur Sozialgeschichte des Neuen Testaments* (Munich, 1990), 250–51.

18. At that time, the number of women among Christian believers was apparently greater than that of men. The correction of the text in D05 Cantabrigiensis is, as quite frequently in Acts, interested to make independent women look like appendages of men (or of their husbands). It says, "and among the prominent *men and women* many...," instead of saying, "and of the prominent Greek *women and men* not a few."

19. See on that, L. Schottroff, "Antijudaismus im Neuen Testament," in *Befreiungserfahrungen*, 217ff.

20. For a Christian argument against circumcision, see the Christian writing from antiquity *De Altercatione Ecclesiae et Synagogae* 42.1131–40, which Brooten points out (*Women Leaders*, 63–64). See the respective Christian argument from modernity in W. D. Thomas, "The Place of Women in the Church at Philippi," *ExpTim* 83 (1972): 117–18; his essay is, as a whole,

a documentation of how women are used in the Christian argumentation against Jewish religion. See also Weiser, "Die Rolle," 167.

21. Kuhn and Stegemann say: "For these [women], the conversion to Judaism was easier than for men since one did not require of women either circumcision or sacrifice" ("Proselyten," 1263). See also G. Schille in his commentary on Acts 13:50.

22. These are the emendations by H. Gunkel, *Esther* (Tübingen, 1913), 96 n. 81 and the Biblia Hebraica Stuttgartensia of Esth. 2:19.

23. Gunkel (*Esther*, 13) uses the phrase "spiced-up girls" to refer to the virgins who, according to harem regulations, had been prepared for the king with ointments for the past twelve months. See Esth. 2:12.

24. Thomas, "Place," 118 n. 1; he gives no explicit reason for this text but only assumes generally that the upper-class women of the Roman Empire had a particular religious interest. Yet one has to differentiate this general picture.

25. S. B. Pomeroy, *Goddesses, Whores, Wives and Slaves* (New York: Schocken Books, 1975); German translation, *Frauenleben im klassischen Altertum* (Stuttgart, 1985), 320.

26. Concerning the Isis cult, see the listing of prohibitions and limitations in Pomeroy, *Frauenleben*, 350–52, and in S. K. Heyob, *The Cult of Isis among Women in the Graeco-Roman World* (Leiden: E. J. Brill, 1975), 18–33. One can disregard here the changed Roman politics under Caligula regarding the Isis cult. In the case of Judaism, one can see the connection between prohibitions and the attraction for women during the expulsion by Tiberius (Josephus, *Ant.* 18.81–84; Suetonius, *Tiberius* 36; Dio Cassius, *Roman History* 57.18.5a; Tacitus, *Ann.* 2.85). Tacitus places the persecution of the Jews in the context of the measures for women's discipline. Thus, the story of the Roman upper-class woman Fulvia, which Josephus tells in this connection, is supplemented and corrected: The point was not the attraction of *one* woman, who was tricked by Jewish "swindlers," but the attraction of Judaism for many Roman women and men. The story of Jews being deceptive is here only an excuse for the persecution of Jews, just as the story of Paulina's scandal is an excuse for the persecution of members

of the Isis cult (Josephus, *Ant.* 18.65–80; Suetonius, *Tiberius* 36; Tacitus, *Ann.* 2.85).

27. Pomeroy, *Frauenleben*, 349.

28. On the Isis cult, see Heyob, *Cult*, 81–110, and the respective chapter in Pomeroy, *Frauenleben;* on Judaism, see Brooten, *Women Leaders*.

29. See the expression concerning the man who lives by himself.

30. See the expression "*more* regarding worship" (*epi pleon*).

31. Brooten, *Women Leaders*, 35–39.

4

Women as Disciples of Jesus in New Testament Times

Women in the Roman Empire, First Century C.E.

The Wealthy Woman

Wealthy, truly independent, upper-class women were common in all regions of the Roman Empire. In spite of differences in their legal situation, their social reality was fairly uniform; and, in spite of some legal limitations, the factual situation of these women was one of nearly unrestricted freedom.[1] In this period, women everywhere owned wealth, administered it independently, and bought assets as businesswomen, even when married. The rich businesswoman and priestess Eumachia of Pompeii was from a powerful, Pompeian family. She owned a centrally situated building with a front that was forty meters wide.[2] She was no exception. In papyrus documents on business life, one finds quite frequent reference to businesswomen, for example the woman landlord of a big trading house (Egypt, 13 B.C.E.),[3] or women who leased land.[4]

Likewise, Jewish women in Egypt owned livestock, land, and vineyards.[5] Suetonius mentions women in Rome who built trade ships.[6] One can take Herodias's story in Mark 6:14–29 as representative of the role of women in the leading families of the Roman Empire. Instances similar to that reported of a woman in Herodias's family are reported by first-century historians concerning women in Roman upper-class families. These women marry into the same class from which they come. They marry many times, often in a quick succession of divorce and remarriage. They use their marriage and their husbands for expanding their areas of influence, and they do not flinch at the sight of a chopped-off head of someone who was in their way. Thus, one can compare Herodias's story in many details with that, for example, of Poppaea Sabina. In her last marriage, Poppaea was the wife of Emperor Nero, and at the height of her success she was presented the cut-off head of her predecessor, Nero's previous wife, Octavia, who had been murdered and against whose dismissal by Nero the Roman populace had protested heavily.[7] If one disregards this exceptional situation of a marriage to a man in political leadership, one can say that upper-class women were—even without equality in the legal sense—partaking fully in the fruits of power and in an independent accumulation of wealth. Even for her cruelty Herodias is representative, though I do not wish to contend here that *all* women of the Roman upper class were cruel. The contemporary Ovid, who is nonpartial on this problem, reminds the women: "You should also leave alone the slave woman; I hate that woman who scratches the female servants' faces and punctures their arms with needles."[8]

Thus, the narrative in Mark 6:14–29 is a story from life (in the upper class). If one adds the independent and well-respected women of whom Luke tells (see below), one can observe that the New Testament also sheds light on the social reality concerning the freedom wealthy women enjoyed. This idea matches the one coming from secular sources.

It is a matter of taste whether one should perceive the relatively unrestricted life of independent businesswomen and of the women of rich and powerful families as an expression of women's liberation. It will depend on how one interprets the meaning of that life. There are no documents as such written by women. In that respect, even these ladies of high society are "silent women."[9] In contrast, these women have frequently an education similar to the men of their social class;[10] they most likely use birth-control methods;[11] they themselves are in charge of their bodies with remarkable sexual freedom; and they are in charge of their fortune (and their slaves). The endless moral complaints of Roman men about the sexual licentiousness of women[12] and, most of all, the kind of behavior of women called for by ethical literature show that, though the so-called emancipation of Roman women was a product of the general wealth of this patriarchal class, ruling the world, it was not accepted in the consciences of most men and moralists. The portrayal of the sexual freedom of women is juxtaposed to an extremely unemancipated women's ideal in literary sources. Even the progressive philosopher Musonius, who holds that daughters be educated in similar fashion as sons, envisions the ideal woman to be one who, after having studied philosophy, is an especially apt housewife in the sense of the Roman ideal: She serves the husband, manages the household, and is, in short, seated by the spinning wheel.[13] To bolster their propaganda for the nostalgic women's ideal, more conservative moralists add enraged utterances about emancipated women. Valerius Maximus says about a woman who always managed her own legal affairs that she was impudent and litigious. He then notes her date of death, commenting: "It is historically more noteworthy when such a monster dies than when it is born."[14] Also to him, the ideal woman is married only once in life,[15] has children for her most beautiful jewels,[16] and knows how to properly express her submission to the man.

Reality in Roman life looks different. Valerius Maximus complains that only the Romans' images of the gods reflect the proper custom of men lying at the table and women sitting in chairs: Jupiter lies on the cushion, while Juno is offered a chair. That picture is different in Roman homes, "perhaps because goddesses are more willing to comply with that strict custom than wives."[17] The contrast between the ethical ideas of the ideal woman and reality—as it has been unearthed by Thraede quite clearly[18]—can be observed on many levels of life. Plutarch recommends to the young wife not to have her own feelings, only those of her husband, and to have the same gods as the husband.[19] However, many upper-class women became, in contrast to such recommendations, active in Oriental religions, which were quite suspect to several men and often to the government. These religions were Judaism, the Isis cult, and then Christianity as it emerged.[20] There is plenty of evidence that women had religions that differed from their husbands'. One could perceive this religious activity as female independence or as an attempt for self-actualization, which had not yet become possible in principle for women of the upper class, in spite of their freedom. At any rate, the contradiction between the ideology of the moral woman and the much more liberal doings of women of wealth is no harmless squabble between the sexes. Instead, the ideology of virtuousness needs to be brought in connection with the ideology of the Roman state.

Limitation of Women's Freedom in the Interest of the State

Everywhere, one can observe the state's interest in the "virtuousness" of women during the first century. Augustus's laws on marriage and family were still followed.[21] The state tried to legislate—though apparently with little success—that more marriages be had in the upper class and more children be raised, and that the family, organized in strict and moral fashion, become the basis of Roman power. Of Augustus's broad reform program and its continuation into the first century, only that aspect will be examined now that concerns the political dimension of the ideology of the role of women. At issue was the politics of populating the empire and, consequently, securing power and maintaining the state's order.

Again, Valerius Maximus says quite clearly: Is a woman permitted to give a public speech? No, if the patriarchal custom (*patrius mos*)—the state constitution, that is—is to be kept. Only when the quiet of the state is disturbed by waves of turmoil will situations occur that for moral women are simply embarrassing.[22]

The connection between the state's politics of order and the ideology of the woman's role is just as clear in Ovid's work. His *Ars amatoria,* instruction in the art of love, which in no way pertains only to marriage, contributed to Ovid's being banned by Augustus as part of a moral cleansing order in 8 B.C.E.[23] Ovid's awareness of the political problem when writing the *Ars amatoria* is obvious from the following shielding contention, which is heterogeneous to the context: "You head cover, stay far from me, you sign of virginity, and you long trimming, covering the feet. Only about assured enjoyment of love and permitted theft do I sing; nowhere in my poem do I teach a crime" (1.31ff.).[24] The virtuous, freeborn wife with her symbols of honor—her head cover of ribbons (*vittae*) and hem ornaments—is asked to plug her ears. Of course, the book could be in no way considered an appeal to commit a crime, to commit adultery, that is, with a free, married woman, or to engage in licentious acts with a free, single woman or widow. At the end, Ovid reassures once again: "I will not disturb the guards of the wife; it is good this way, for virtue, custom, and law say so" (3.611ff.). Political pressure was great, as can be gathered from these defensive statements. The women members of the emperor's family had to publicly represent honor, something the state asked of women, even though in private they did not always keep to these norms. One can observe this double standard of morality even in the case of Livia, Augustus's politically active and powerful wife. Her appearance in public, all the way down to her attire, corresponded, without doubt, with Augustus's ideas and represented the purity of virtue in the home, which was to match the "old tradition."[25] Her love affair before her marriage to Augustus certainly did not correspond with this kind of morality, since the affair started while Livia was still married—and Livia was pregnant on top of it.[26]

In addition, Livia was most certainly not the wife who was obedient to her husband, as she was supposed to be according to moral standards.[27] In similar fashion, Poppaea Sabina appears to have presented herself in public as especially virtuous—with her face half-veiled—in spite of her emancipated life-style.[28]

The political dimension of the ideals of womanhood propagated in the Roman state, for which one can find even further evidence,[29] is so evident that one cannot consider even tombstones, on which frequently these ideals were enumerated, as naive documents of private life. One says: "She was an incomparable wife, a good mother, an honorable grandmother, chaste, pious, hardworking, well-behaved, energetic, alert, caring, only one man's loyal wife, a house mother full of diligence and reliability."[30] With this stone, another of the various public confessions to the state's order has been added.

Hence, the "emancipation" of Roman upper-class women is an ambiguous matter. On the one hand, wealth allowed women great possibilities; on the other, the pillars of the state's order tried to repress these freedoms and to fight them with a backward-looking ideology. The ambiguity cannot be explained based on the economic situation of the Roman upper class. In his economics book, Xenophon (ca. 430–354 B.C.E.) describes a landowner who educates his young wife to become the administrator of his home. She has to raise the children and to supervise the work that needs to be done in the house. The husband has his own administrator, whom he himself has educated and with whom he works.[31] In the first century C.E., Columella wrote a primer on farming that presupposes circumstances that are a lot more spacious than those described by Xenophon. The estates of the Roman upper class at Columella's time comprise vast stretches of land. The owner lives in the city and looks after the property only once in a while. The care of the estate is entrusted to tenants and overseers (see *De re rustica*, esp. 1.8). It is obvious that under such conditions a woman caretaker has to be hired for all work to be done in the house (ibid., 12.1ff.), just as had been done many generations earlier in Cato's time (*De agri cultura* 10–11). Although Columella mentions the cause for this change in regard to Xenophon's economy (the owners no longer live on the estate) and that the change has effects on *both* sexes, he cannot avoid attacking the laziness and self-indulgence of Roman *women*, "since in general this old spirit of Sabinic and Roman landladies not only has become old-fashioned, but has vanished totally."[32] In reality, not even the clothes of the slaves are totally produced on the estate itself.[33] Yet he reproaches the landlady for no longer doing any wool work (*lanificium*).

The harshness and proliferation of these disciplinary

attempts, at first mainly directed at the women of the upper class, are astounding. In Columella's case, one can easily see that true, economic reasons are not present for such demands on women. After all, the system he decries has been working well for several generations. In itself, his book is—as an instruction for administering large estates—a proof of this fact. The reason for the strong public emphasis on the traditional role of the woman is that the leading men in the Roman Empire greatly fear a political endangerment of the state's order. Cato (in Livius) argues in an explicitly political manner also; he speaks of *seditio* and *secessio,* upheaval and secession (Livius 34.5.5), because women as a whole are standing up publicly for a cause that concerns them. Valerius Maximus goes back to this instance (*Factorum Dictorumque Memorabilium Libri* 9.1.3). He laments that men back then did not imagine "where this audacity, once having gained victory over the laws, would lead." A Stoic philosopher of the second century B.C.E. speaks of "anarchy" that is spreading because men are not marrying and thus are not educating their wives strictly for their roles as women.[34]

The political backdrop of the official Roman ideal of women is also apparent in conflicts between Christians and the Roman state in the second century. One gleans from a letter by Pliny the Younger to Trajan that during the examinations of Christians or former Christians, both the question whether they commit crimes and the question whether their assemblies are endangering the state are discussed.[35] Political crimes and misdemeanors are here not distinguished. Adulteries (*adulteria*) are also listed as crimes. It is likely that the list of (noncommitted) crimes was not defined by the persons examined but by the Roman government. The examined are with great certainty not Roman citizens, as one can see from the general context of the letter. Thus, it can be concluded, first, that the declaration that one did not commit adulteries is not too far away from declaring one's loyalty to the state and, second, that the circle of people for whom the strict public moral order of Rome was meant was much larger than it was at first with Augustus's legislation on marriage. Defamation through sexual libertinism and through offending the incest laws is used also, according to Athenagoras, to incite the government to especially harsh procedures against Christians.[36]

The Working Woman and the Poor Woman

Most people of the Roman Empire were hardworking, if not to say poor, people. It is, however—due to the scarce sources about them—much more difficult to find out about their situation than about that of the rich. It is even more difficult to find information on those women working in mines, on farms, and in low service positions than it is on men in these same situations. There were, indeed, also women among the most miserable—the slaves in mines.[37]

Women also worked in farming. This fact becomes obvious in Columella, though somewhat tangentially. Whenever he speaks of the desirable physical condition of slaves working in the field, he does not mention women. Likewise, the description of the various farm jobs gives the impression that work in the field was performed only by men. But concerning the duties of the *villica*, the female administrator, he says: "In order to keep women busy with wool work on rainy days or when they cannot perform work during cold or frost out in the field, one should also have unkempt wool in store, so that through spinning or weaving they can easier do their share of work time."[38] This passage shows not only that women worked in the fields but also that the specific woman's role, defined by the ideal virtues of women, did definitely not apply to women slaves. After all, a little earlier Columella says (as many others before and after him): The deity has destined the man "to suffer heat and frost, to endure journeys and pains in both peace and war, in farming and in military service"; the woman, however, is destined to the care of household matters.[39] Based on Columella, one can formulate the additional hypothesis: Whenever there is talk about the work of slaves—and probably also about hard, lowly work of free people—women are not particularly mentioned, though they are part of it. The differentiation between the sexes becomes, from the standpoint of the authors, apparently marginal.[40] For that reason, one finds out only accidentally that women were even among slaves who had been tied by ropes and used for farming.[41] The Italian circumstances, which Columella describes here, are no exception to the rule. One will have to assume that in the provinces of the Roman Empire, also in Palestine, women were working in the fields. This fact is underlined by the existence of Greek words for women doing such work: *hē erithos*—the female day laborer; *kalamētris*—the female collector of ears of grain; *theristria*—the female cutter; *poastria*—the female weeder; *trygētria*—the female helper in the vineyard; *phyganistria*—the female collector of wood.[42] Also Jewish women worked in the field.[43]

Material on the work of women in service positions is much easier to come by than material on farm work, since tombstone inscriptions document the former to a great extent. Women deal with goods of daily need: nails, lead, beans, perfume, fish, barley. They are bakers, confectioners, hostesses of taverns, silk weavers, hairstylists, lime-burners, makers of ointments, stenographers, and repeatedly midwives and doctors (doctors and midwives probably are hardly differentiated).[44] Within the *familia* of rich men or women, many slaves or former slaves work in service positions related to the home.[45]

Examining the wages of women is most successful where they appear in relation to men's wages. A papyrus from Egypt (third century B.C.E.) contains an entry by a group of weavers with a plea for a raise. They can no longer live on three drachma for one piece of linen. The entry says, "For each piece of linen it takes three men and one woman, and in six days we are ready to cut it off.... Give each of us [an extra] one and a half obolos and to the woman half an obolos."[46] It can be assumed that the weavers also share the wages per piece in this fashion so that the woman earns a third of the man's wages. Overall, this kind of work seems to pay very little. The pay raise is comparable to the woman's having an additional half loaf of bread over a period of six days. A similar picture is gained from *Diocletian's Maximal Tariff* (301 C.E.). A female weaver of rough material receives twelve denarii per day and food, and with finer material sixteen denarii. The male linen weaver receives for "lowly work" twenty denarii in addition to food; next to shepherding, weaving is the worst-paying male job. A linen weaver of finer materials earns forty denarii as opposed to sixteen denarii for the woman, who does the same work.[47] It is "remarkable that the wages of the female weaver, even when working with wool, remain time wages, although the male wool weaver is paid by the piece"; hence the woman "has less wage categories available, and the wage differences for fine and rough work are less than for the male weavers."[48] At the same time, a shirt "of rough linen for use among common women or slaves"—that is, of the third (lowest) quality—costs five hundred denarii (*Diocletian's Maximal Tariff* 26.31–33), and one modius (17.5 liters) of barley costs one hundred denarii (ibid., 1.2).

The situation of craftswomen can be seen primarily in the case of loan contracts: They often are contract partners with their husbands and are then also liable for the payments.[49] The craftscouple Prisca and Aquila, who were fairly important for the spread of the gospel of Christ, should be imagined as typical for craftscouples of their society: They work together. This fact can be deduced from the texts of the New Testament (Acts 18:3). Paul, Prisca, and Aquila work together as *skēnopoioi*. Although it is not clear which craft was meant, it is clear from Paul's comments (1 Cor. 4:12; 1 Thess. 2:9) that it was a strenuous craft.[50]

Women as Disciples of Jesus

Women in the Jesus Movement in Palestine

The Gospel of Luke is the only New Testament text that takes interest in our subject. Luke mentions the women who follow Jesus already in his report of Jesus' journey through Palestine (Luke 8:1–3; see also 10:38–42). In the Gospels of Mark and Matthew, however, the women emerge almost out of nowhere and as late as in the context of the reports on the passion and the resurrection: Now, it is quickly added that these women have already been following Jesus in Galilee (Mark 15:40–41; Matt. 27:55–56). In Mark's and Matthew's accounts of Jesus' life up to his death, the women who are around Jesus are especially among the people on whom Jesus performs miracles (i.e., Peter's mother-in-law, the woman letting blood).

In spite of this source situation, one has to read particularly the Gospel of Luke on our question with special care. That is so because Luke has formed in his Gospel a very specific image of the women's role in the Jesus movement, and that image is historically inaccurate in decisive points: He imagines that the apostles left their wives in order to follow Jesus (Luke 14:26; 18:29) and that the women following Jesus on his way are at least in part members of wealthy families and are supporting Jesus' followers "out of their wealth" (Luke 8:3). He is enthralled by the celibacy of the apostles, whom he imagines as ascetic, Kynic itinerant evangelists.[51] His idea that wealthy women were close to Jesus does not originate from otherwise lost traditions of the Jesus movement but from later experiences of the young church in the cities of the Roman Empire outside Palestine, which Luke projects back into Jesus' time (see Acts 16:14–15; 17:4, 12).[52]

One need not doubt, however, that already during the Jesus movement in Palestine, women joined Jesus' disciples on their journeys. The self-evident and casual mentioning of this occurrence in Mark 15:40–41 and Matt. 27:55–56 speaks for that. A few further conclusions concerning these women and their situation are warranted, on the one hand, because of texts from the Logia source (sayings source Q) and the oldest tradition about Jesus, deducible from the former;[53] and, on the other, because of pre-Markan traditions.

In the Logia source as in the oldest Jesus tradition, which can be deduced from the former, the situation of women as disciples of Jesus is not thematized; their participation, however, is quietly presupposed. Whenever there is talk of "the poor, the blind, the lame," and so on, both men and women are meant. One should imagine the grotesque picture that would result from assuming that in Jesus' beatitudes on the poor only the poor *men* are meant. Both men and women are healed and, hence, are following Jesus. One could conclude from Matt. 11:1–5, a text that comprehensively describes both the situation of the oldest Jesus movement and the time of the Logia source, that during the Jesus movement in Palestine neither groups of people nor certain of their functions are strictly distinguished. Men and women are not distinguished, and the group of the sick are not distinguished from the group of the poor. The proclamation of the gospel of the poor and that of the healing of the sick belong together. One can assume that during this time, every follower of Jesus received with the gift of discipleship also the task of proclamation and healing. The commissioning of the disciples in the old saying of Matt. 10:7–8 does not make the disciples an exclusive group that stands apart from the group of Jesus' followers who do not receive such a commissioning. Although there might already be talk here of the Twelve, one has to understand such talk as representative for all those who follow Jesus. Hence, one can conclude from Matt. 11:2–5 par. that Luke (in Luke 8:2) describes the Jesus movement in Palestine accurately when he states that women followed Jesus and were healed by him. One could add that this following involved the proclamation of the message that the kingdom of God was at hand.

The fact that women as disciples of Jesus are not mentioned in the texts that can be traced back to the Jesus movement of Palestine can be explained by the androcentrism of language and the "equality" that poverty produces. This situation can be best recognized in the hope-centered contents of this movement. The misery of the poor is to be ended; they hope for tables covered with food, which God will prepare for them and which will fill them up (Luke 6:20–21; Luke 1:53). It is self-evident that women, men, and children will participate in God's banquet; hence, from an androcentric perspective, one need not mention this explicitly since now women, men, and children share the same hardship. It is only later—in the Pauline communities of faith, where absolute indigence is no longer a leading problem—that the removal of the dominance gap between man and woman becomes a message of hope (Gal. 3:28) within the framework of the androcentric perspective. The "equality" produced by hardship can, by the way, also be recognized in the situation of the poor and working women, which was portrayed earlier in this chapter. Even on the journey of the indigent, their "flight for social reasons,"[54] one meets not only men without families (Job 24:5, 12). The women of the rebellious Jews, who threw everything "they could lay their hands on" from their housetops (Josephus, *BJ* 3.303) on the heads of Vespasian's troops in Jerusalem, also acted from an "equality" produced by hardship.

The circumstances in which the large patriarchal families lived are a thing of the past for the rather poor followers of Jesus. Clearly they have come to know that Jesus' message separates families and that disciples of Jesus are forced to leave their families (the large patriarchal family, that is) (Matt. 10:34–37 par.; Matt. 8:21–22 par.). They feel that the rupture of the families is an expression of apocalyptic hardship, a sign that the end is near. Only from a distance are they familiar with the life of those still in complete families and in some luxury:

> For as the days of Noah were, so will be the coming of the Son of Man. For as in those days before the flood they were eating and drinking, marrying and giving in marriage [their daughters, that is], until the day Noah entered the ark, and they knew nothing until the flood came and swept them all away. (Matt. 24:37–39)

In these very persuasive and visual words, the entire situation becomes quite clear: The followers of Jesus stand dismayed outside the houses of those who can lead a "normal" (and in their eyes an even "rich") life, having food and families. This apparently normal life expresses ignorance and indifference. The male and female followers of Jesus have tried to no avail to awaken the others, to win them over, to proclaim to them that judgment day is near. "But you resisted" (Matt. 23:37 par.). Here are people who, because of poverty and the prospect of further pauperization, see the world of unbroken families and of sufficient food supplies as one filled with ignorance of reality and the future. They are almost desperate to open the deaf ears of those who are rejecting their message. Underlying this text, one senses the dismay over why people could want to be so ignorant. And indeed, it must have taken quite a bit of egotism and indifference to remain during that time unfazed by reality and the threat of the future—the economic misery of a large section of the Jewish people and the touchy political situation preceding the Jewish-Roman War. The messengers of Jesus preached conversion, and together they built their lives on a hope in God. The community, built on the hope of God's kingdom, is not the family but the togetherness of Jesus' followers, the *familia Dei* (see Mark 3:31–35 par.). Divorces, however, appear not to play a role here—in distinction to the destruction of the extended family as it existed then; they are not mentioned as a problem within the group of Jesus' followers.[55] The disciple who leaves his family does not thereby abandon his wife (see Matt. 10:34–37 par.; Matt. 8:21 par.; cf. also Mark 10:29 against Luke 14:26; 18:29). Men who for social reasons do not settle down and leave their families in their former place of residence do not regard their marriages, even outside the Jesus movement, as dissolved.[56] The rule might be, however, that the poor leaving their wives and children out of destitution do not return. With whatever skepticism the followers of Jesus looked upon the life of the extended family, they were strongly committed to the community of the *familia Dei* (see only Mark 10:42–45) and the relationship between man and woman—a relationship that was not defined in terms of setting up a family and having children.

Also in this instance, the picture resulting from the Logia source with its oldest Jesus tradition harmonizes with the pre-Markan narrative in Mark 10:2–9. The relationship between a man and a woman is here presented in the evocative language of utopia: God has created both of them "from the beginning of creation" as two human beings, whose togetherness brings to an end common experience (or the natural laws). They "are no longer two, but *one* flesh" (Mark 10:6–9). The union as *mia sarx* is not defined by sexual intercourse but by sharing each other's life for good (see 9:6–7 with relation to divorce practice). Creation is mentioned here to express a message of hope.

One could also say that the two will become one flesh in the reign of God. Life, which springs from God's hand (whether by God's doing as creator or as eschatological ruler over Israel), is of an almost unlimited perfection to Jesus' followers. These people, marked by poverty, look at the plants and rejoice that the lives of plants are only a small indication of God's care they themselves receive (Matt. 6:25-33 par.). These people live with their wives under conditions marked by dirt, sickness, and homelessness; yet they perceive themselves as Adam and Eve, as two equal people in the sense of perfect creation and unity.

This perfect dream most certainly also influenced these people's practical lives, since we can see also in other respects that their hopes were turned into concrete experiences of happiness together (as, for example, in the healing of the sick). However, one should not view this practice as implying a *prohibition* of divorce that intends to force a woman or man who wants to dissolve a marriage to maintain this marriage in the name of God and Jesus. The positive concept of community, present here, forbids such a thought, and so does a reflection on the concrete situation. In Mark 10:2-9 God's will for creation is contrasted with the reality of God's people. The command of a divorce letter by Moses makes sense and is necessary in light of hard reality (Mark 10:5). The law to issue a divorce letter, hence, is not dissolved. Besides, it would have been the worst that could have happened to the women. After all, the letter of divorce secured for the divorced woman certain financial future perspectives and guaranteed her the right of entering a new marriage. Hence, one should not view Mark 10:2-9 as a prohibition of divorce so as to protect the woman from the man's arbitrariness. Likewise, one should not perceive the text as an expression of Christian ideas on marriage in contrast to Jewish practice. The text is addressed to Israel as a whole since all of Israel is hard-hearted. The end of all hopes, expressed in this text—and the end of the hopes among Jesus' messengers—is the reconstruction of creation as the salvation of *entire* Israel. Jesus' messengers see themselves as Jews who are expressing God's will for all of Israel. So the text is by no means a Magna Carta of Christian marriage and family ethics implying that the foremost meaning of family is the raising of children. The passage of Gen. 1:28 ("be fruitful and multiply") is purposely not mentioned in the text; neither does the text encourage people to enter marriage.

The different situation of women and men is not an issue in the Jesus movement of Palestine since experience is determined by the equality that poverty and the common hope of God's kingdom produce. Perhaps the situation of women is described only in one way, namely when their lives highlight the hardship of the poor in an especially clear way: in the case of prostitutes and of the woman "letting blood." The fate of prostitutes is primarily a result of poverty or enslavement. Matthew 21:31 constitutes a kind of beatitude for prostitutes and has to be considered as one of the oldest traditions.[57] The pre-Markan narrative of the woman "letting blood" (Mark 5:25–34) tells of a woman whose sickness involves also social isolation: Not only in Judaism but also in antiquity in general, menstruation or bleeding sicknesses of women were considered dangerous for everyone nearby. Things touched by such a woman become unclean (Lev. 15:19–33; *Zabim* 5:6);[58] the woman is not allowed to participate in the Passover (Josephus, *BJ* 6.426–27).

In these contexts, menstruation, leprosy, and women's diseases are viewed as similar problems. The woman touches Jesus in order to get well by the touch. As the woman touches Jesus secretly on the back of his cloak, it makes no difference whether she is embarrassed about her disease or whether she knows that her touch will make Jesus unclean.[59] The isolated situation of this woman is already created by a certainly common superstition, as mentioned by Pliny the Elder: "Cider which they approach in this condition turns sour;...plants in the yard shrivel up, and the fruits of trees on which they sat drop off; ... ore and even iron become afflicted by rust, and the air is filled with a repulsive odor."[60] These traditional views, which I know even from my own time when growing up in the country, and the purification laws for a Jewish woman of Lev. 15:15ff. suffice to make the situation of this woman equal to that of a leper. The people who reported this story were aware of the situation of a woman with such a disease. Jesus does not reproach or blame this woman. Hence, he acts differently than the people who had any dealings with her. He affirms through his word (Mark 5:34) the magical, miraculous happening that has already occurred.

The story of Jesus' encounter with the woman letting blood tells, on the one hand, of the great faith of the woman in Jesus' wonderful power; on the other hand, it tells of the human dignity that women letting blood have in the eyes of Jesus (and his followers). When considering the context of magical thinking, in which this story in particular is narrated (especially the idea of Jesus' power to work wonders [5:29]), it becomes clear that superstition is not overcome here by intellectual enlightenment but by the hope of God's kingdom, which eliminates that women be discriminated against (out of superstition) due to their physical condition. The utopic idea of what a person is according to God's will has more force to dispel the concrete hardship of this woman than the studies of medicine in Alexandria,[61] on condition that people like Jesus and his followers turn this utopia into reality—as in this miracle account.

Mark 15:40 states about women as disciples of Jesus in Palestine that they served (*diakonein*) him. Although much speaks for viewing these lines as Markan,[62] it is still necessary to question that conclusion. Luke had financial support in mind when referring to the service women offered to Jesus and his followers (8:1-3; on the fact that this idea does not hold true for the situation of the Jesus movement in Palestine, see above). If Mark had, indeed, thought that the women's service constituted providing and preparing meals—after the fashion of Peter's mother-in-law, who entertained Jesus and the disciples (Mark 1:31)—he most certainly would not have said: "They served *him* [Jesus]" (15:41). Besides, this situation is hardly conceivable: Jesus, the disciples, and his group of women travel from Galilee to Jerusalem. How should one imagine the women providing and preparing the food in the midst of this scene? One can assume that the service the women offered Jesus be understood as a *diakonia Christou:* They were his messengers and were commissioned;[63] "serving" and "following" are here mutually complementing and explanatory terms. Hence, Mark presupposes with amazing ease that the women in Palestine were commissioned also for the service of proclamation.

A few later handwritten documents have omitted the note "they served him." Especially the Codex Bezae Cantabrigiensis tries here, as also in other places of Acts, to retract the role of women in early Christianity by little changes of the text.[64] A reflection on the specific woman's role takes place in Mark (or in pre-Markan tradition) in neither positive nor negative fashion. Just as carefree as the service of proclamation is mentioned, so it is reported that Peter's mother-in-law wanted to cook for and entertain Jesus and his disciples in order to demonstrate that she had been healed (Mark 1:31). It may be doubtful whether the women in the oldest Jesus movement had such disposition over their homes and food. The carefree spirit of equality that existed among the disciples of Jesus and that speaks from Mark 15:40–41, and also the carefree stance vis-à-vis the traditional role of women, should depict the situation of the Jesus movement in Palestine accurately.

The correctness of the above picture concerning the role of women as disciples of Jesus in Palestine prior to 70 C.E. is confirmed by the tradition of the women at Jesus' tomb (Mark 15:47–16:8). One should ask first what meaning their behavior has in the overall context of Mark's Gospel. Before Jesus' death, the disciples have fled during his arrest (14:50), and Peter has denied him (14:71). They are afraid—as Mark had said of them earlier while they were still journeying with Jesus (4:40; 8:16, 32; 10:32). Jesus dies, deserted by everyone. Now, all of a sudden, Mark mentions the women. They look at the cross from afar (15:40); they see where Jesus is buried (15:47); they go to the tomb to embalm the body (16:1). And then, in a terrible repetition, the same thing happens to the women as to the men before: They run away and are full of fear (16:8). The message of the angel after Jesus' resurrection fills them with fear in the same way as the disciples were filled with fear when hearing Jesus' prophesies concerning his passion and resurrection. Although Mark may have used an older tradition for this portrayal of the disciples' fear and the ensuing fear of the women, it is still clear how important this failure of Jesus' followers is for his writing of the Gospel story. One will have to explain Mark's view of the disciples from the situation of Mark's community of faith, which fears having to face the same fate as Jesus' (see only 8:34–36; 13:12) and whose fear Mark takes very seriously. He tells the members of his community of faith the story about the fear of the disciples, the fear of the women, and the fear of Jesus (15:34). And he encourages them to accept their fear and continue their path of discipleship. The suffering Jesus is the Son of God (15:39), and the cowardly Peter and the fearful disciples have become the proclaimers of Jesus' resurrection.

The frightened women soon broke their silence, although all that is not explicitly mentioned. Mark tells of the fear of the disciples and the women since he is clearly aware that they have become the proclaimers of the gospel. Mark 16:8 may be the original ending of the Gospel of Mark; however, for Mark and for the church(es) for which he writes, the event referred to in that verse is not the end of the gospel proclamation but the beginning of the disciples' work after Jesus' death.

Hence, Mark presupposes the proclamation of the female and male disciples after Jesus' death, and he does not see the women as having a more particular role than the male disciples: The women have failed just as the men and will pass on the gospel just as they.[65]

From what is portrayed by the Gospel of Mark, one can draw various conclusions concerning the pre-Markan tradition and the actual role of women in the Jesus movement of Palestine. The fact that Mark uses different lists of names (15:40, 47; 16:1) points to a pre-Markan tradition. In this context, Mary Magdalene has a fixed role: She is mentioned each time and each time in the first place. Mark has no apparent interest in that only women stand by Jesus' tomb. This, too, is most likely based on such tradition. One can conclude from Mark 15:47–16:8 that a group of women played a decisive role in passing on the message of God's kingdom. The fact that Mary Magdalene was in this group seems to have been remembered quite firmly by the reporters. The fact that here, all at once, women act as an isolated group speaks for the age of this tradition: There is no other reason to speak of these women than the memory of the actual account. The angel's message to the women is in Mark also—in spite of the women's failure—a commissioning to proclaim the resurrection, which Mark sees them eventually fulfill. The story of the epiphany to Mary Magdalene and other women, a story in which they are commissioned in Mark 16:1–8, is a pre-Markan tradition. Just as Jesus with his later appearances prompted many people to proclaim him (1 Cor. 15:3–8), so the angel by the empty tomb commissioned the women to proclamation. There is no use in arguing over the time priority here concerning the commissioning of the women by the epiphany of the angel versus the appearance of Jesus to Peter—neither is there use in arguing over the rank of these messengers of Jesus. However, the isolated role of the women in Mark 15:47–

16:8 speaks for the assumption that after Jesus' death, a time came when the men among the followers had lost their courage and the women were beginning to continue the work. Matthew even reports Jesus' appearance to women (Matt. 28:9–10). In Luke, the women carry out the instruction of the angel (24:9–10). In the Gospel of John, it is not Mary Magdalene who is commissioned at the tomb, and it is Peter and the Beloved Disciple who see the empty grave (John 20:6–8). Still, Mary Magdalene has the first encounter with the Jesus of the epiphanies and carries out the order of proclamation (20:18). Besides Mark 15:47–16:8, no additional information can be gleaned from the other Gospels concerning the situation in Palestine at the time. Whether the epiphany in the context of which the women were commissioned involved an angel or Jesus was probably irrelevant to those experiencing it.

In Paul's description of epiphanies occurring after Jesus' death, the women are missing (1 Cor. 15:3–8). That simply means that 1 Cor. 15:3–8 is the earliest Christian testimony that Christian men no longer dared to admit how important the work of women had been for the proclamation of the gospel. The contradiction between the factual importance of women in the Christian communities and the statements (or the absence of such) about it in Christian texts becomes more and more apparent (see more below) especially in Paul. The fact that the women are not mentioned in 1 Cor. 15:3–8 is almost less astonishing than the fact that they are mentioned in all four Gospel accounts. It is not quite correct to say that the role of women as proclaimers of the Easter message was concealed because women could not be witnesses in court according to Jewish law,[66] and because, hence, their message of the resurrection could not be considered effective in outer circles. The concealment of women in the further—particularly extra-Palestinian—development of Christianity is not based on this specifically Jewish legal concept but on the broader social and political tendencies, primarily outside Palestine, that were aimed at limiting the freedom of women (see more on this below).[67]

The disciples' disbelief of the women's Easter message, which later Christian tradition likes to report on (Luke 24:11; Mark 16:10–11; *Epistle of the Apostles* 10–11), is not due to the fact that the disciples do not want to believe the women because they are women. Instead, the disciples cannot believe any longer that Jesus still is the liberator of Israel since he had died after all (see Luke 24:20–21). And their disbelief does not stop once they see the empty tomb (Luke 24:24). Also the second ending of Mark does not intend to convey that women as women were unworthy of belief to the disciples. (In Mark 16:12, they do not believe male witnesses either; see also 16:14.) In the *Epistle of the Apostles,* Jesus sends two women, one after another, as his messengers. The disciples do not believe them and still do not believe even when Jesus himself goes to see them. Much of the doubt and hardship of later Christian generations is contained in such stories. For the role of women in the context of first-century Christianity, such stories have relevancy only insofar as the idea that women cannot be believed *as women, does not* come into play here. So, rather than having documents of women's repression, we have here documents that show the importance of women for the proclamation at the end of the first century and beyond. One can best observe this paradox of early Christianity through Paul's writings and those after him: the natural and relevant role of women, on the one hand, accompanied by attempts to conceal the women's importance or to push women into the traditional role of submission, on the other.

Interpreters have been saying for a long time that the enumeration of Jesus' appearances in 1 Cor. 15:3–8 is a much older resurrection account than the one in Mark 16:1–8, and that Mark 16:1–8 explains why the news of the empty tomb took so long to spread: because the women kept quiet.[68] This view of tradition development does not take into account the importance of Mark 16:8 in the context of the Gospel of Mark; it also does not explain sufficiently why, all of a sudden, a narrative emerges that describes an angelic appearance to the women at Jesus' tomb. Referring to the empty tomb does not prove the fact of the resurrection, for the empty tomb proves nothing (see Luke 24:24). This view of tradition development is also unable to explain why especially women play a role in this context. Thus, one might say with some historical probability: After the death of Jesus, it was initially women who went about proclaiming Jesus' message about the coming kingdom of God, and they expressed their hope for life by proclaiming that the one crucified was risen. They received strength for this step from the vision that had made them proclaimers of the message that told of the power of life over death. There is no doubt that the equality that was born from poverty and the hope in God's reign, which was taken as a matter of course, contributed to the women in the early Jesus movement taking on so decisive a function.

A similar assessment of the women's situation in the early Jesus movement derives from contemporary evidence showing the importance of Mary, the mother of Jesus. Mary is not honored for being Jesus' mother since family ties are relativized among the followers of Jesus (Mark 3:31–35; see also above). However, Mary's Magnificat (Luke 1:46–54) in its present form most certainly dates back to the oldest Jesus movement.[69] In this psalm, Mary is a symbol of how the lowly are elevated, a symbol of how God will feed the hungry and make them laugh and of how God is already doing so: A poor woman has become the mother of Israel's Messiah, in whose name the messengers proclaim the arrival of the kingdom of God. She *represents as a woman the hope of the poor*—men and women—and not just the hope of women alone.

The self-evident communal spirit among, or the equality of, women and men in the Jesus movement of Palestine has often been contrasted with the drastically patriarchal sayings of Jewish rabbis on the role of women. A favored procedure is to contrast Jesus' behavior with the saying of Hillel: "Many women, much sorcery" or the prohibition, "Do not talk much with a woman."[70] Such comparisons are rather haphazard: It certainly remains open which *practice* existed in dealings with women whenever such *opinions* were uttered—something to which Klaus Thraede has rightly called our attention.[71] In addition, it would be easy to obtain the reverse effect by, for example, placing Christian opinions such as 1 Tim. 2:11–15 in contrast to ideas of the philosopher Musonius. Then, one would see a black-and-white picture that speaks against Christianity. A comparison appears methodologically warranted only if one kind of practice or opinion is compared to another kind of practice or opinion in whose context it belongs and to which it relates. That means that the liberation of men and women as disciples of Jesus out of enslavement by hunger and disease has to be viewed against the backdrop of the concrete living conditions of these people. They tried to free themselves from the plight of poverty. The liberation from patriarchal structures was what people longed for on account of their poverty and resulted from their hope in the reign of God. Yet the rule of men over women was not the primary problem and did not become a topic of discussion. At the center of all proclamation stood the hope of the poor.

Women in the Christian Churches Associated with Paul and Luke

Paul

The authentic letters of Paul leave an ambiguous impression of the role of women in the churches. On the one hand, women have equal functions in the church;

on the other, one finds Pauline opinions on the role of women that ask for hierarchic-patriarchal structures with remarkable hardness.[72] The ambiguous picture Paul conveys is upheld, by the way, until at least the second century. One has to be methodologically precise when distinguishing between information concerning the factual situation of women in the churches and the opinions as to which role women should play. The factual situation of women in the Pauline churches—in the Christian communities situated in the cities of the Roman Empire outside Palestine—becomes especially apparent in the greeting list of Romans 16. (Space does not permit our taking up the question of whether the addressed church was in Rome or Ephesus.)

Paul names in this greeting list individual persons and groups of people, two groups of Christians (house churches? [vv. 14–15]) and groups of slaves or those who had been freed (on Aristobulus and Narcissus, see vv. 10–11). It is unlikely that there were rich people in Paul's churches, unless as a rare exception. The churches, however, are not "poor" in the sense of being destitute (such as the *ptōchoi*). The living standard is in general similar to that of Paul and of Prisca and Aquila: Overall, these people live from their craft or do dependent labor; hence, they are poor people (*penētes*) from the standpoint of the rich.[73] As is obvious from Paul's list of slaves and freed slaves—but also from the use of their proper names—slaves and freed slaves are not a minority in the church addressed in Rom. 16:3–4.[74] Persis, for example, "the Persian woman," is the name of a slave.

When trying to evaluate Paul's greeting list in respect to the situation of women, one can make important observations that clarify the situation of women to a great extent. Of the Christians mentioned by name, nine are women and seventeen men. In this count, Junia (v. 7) is considered a woman. One can now view it only as a curiosity of theological history that, contrary to philological evidence, Junia has frequently been declared to be a man on the basis of no other information than that Junia is called an apostle.[75] The majority of the people are identified more specifically by what they are doing for the churches. In these identifications, one finds a hierarchy neither among men nor between men and women. There clearly are no tasks specifically assigned to women in the church. The work of the couples Prisca and Aquila and Andronicus and Junia is characterized as work done together (vv. 4, 7). Women labored hard for the church (*kopian,* vv. 8, 12)—*kopian* being a word Paul uses also for his own work (1 Thess. 1:3). Women as well as men are called "coworkers" (v. 3; see also v. 9). Women are called "beloved" (see v. 9, "male beloved"). Women experience the same fate as men due to their faith in Christ: They risk their own necks for others (v. 4) and, like Paul, end up in prison (v. 7).

Even apart from the greeting list of Rom. 16:3–16, one can, based on the epistles of Paul, reconstruct the same view of the situation of women. They are among the prophets of the community of faith (1 Cor. 11:4); they are called *diakonos* the same as men (see Phoebe, Rom. 16:1–2; see also Phil. 1:1), and one need not think here of work specifically designed for women. Paul says about two women in Philippi that they fought together with him (Phil. 4:2–3). Paul adds the esteemed title *prostatis* in Phoebe's case to honor her for her services both to him and to many others (Rom. 16:1–2).[76] Paul probably asks the church hosting her to offer her the same extensive hospitality as she had offered to others earlier (Rom. 16:1–2; a hosting man, Rom. 16:23). This fact, by the way, does not speak for her being particularly wealthy.

One can add to this picture easily that of a woman called apostle. There definitely is no difference made between women and men in regard to their work and importance for the building of the churches and, hence, for the proclamation of life and hope.

Paul mentions family members, but only if they, too, have become Christians. Of the nine women on the greeting list in Rom. 16:3–16, four women are named independently without their family members. One can assume that women became Christians without their male family heads—just as slaves were part of the church without their masters. Even before Paul's work, women were at work as part of the "mission" outside Palestine (see Rom. 16:7; that may also be true for Prisca). The characteristics Paul adds to persons in his greeting list indicate a natural and unconstrained equality among the sexes, an equality resulting from the context of Christian faith and practice.

The impression is completely different when examining the opinions Paul utters on the role of the woman. It is true that he hopes that in Christ the structures of domination and dividing differences will be removed (Gal. 3:28), which certainly means to him that the equality of the future is to be lived already in the present, namely within the Christian community. However, Paul contradicts himself when it comes to concrete situations. This problem is most obvious in 1 Cor. 11:2–16. Still, when Paul advocates the woman's submission to the man, one finds a side remark (1 Cor. 11:11ff.) that tries to express the eschatological equality and partnership of man and woman. This side remark, however, is not in keeping with the rest of what he says. In 1 Cor. 11:2–16, Paul presents a massive argument to prompt women to express their submission to the man by wearing head covers during worship service and when praying and prophesying. Paul enlists creation itself in his argument: The woman is created from the man's rib and is his helper (1 Cor. 11:8–9). He calls upon the overall moral perception (v. 6, "reproachful"; v. 13, "proper") and nature (vv. 14–15; in reality, vv. 14–15 are from today's perspective no argument in terms of nature, but of convention). Most of all, however, he argues from a hierarchical power structure: God—Christ—man—woman (v. 3).[77]

From the context of the overall argument, a clear meaning arises for the much-discussed word *exousia*, verse 10: It signifies metonymically the head cover, which means that the woman is supposed to appear with covered head (*katakalyptō tē kephalē*) and, hence, to demonstrate and dramatize that she has a power over her, namely the man, who protects her from the (sexual?) attack of the angels in the cult. Although this situation is clear in the Pauline text, it is difficult to explain the factual everyday custom in Corinth (and elsewhere); it may be that the custom of Christian women in Corinth has rootage in the history of religion, and yet it is still difficult to determine the social significance of the custom that Paul seeks to implement. Depending on how the everyday custom in particular is weighed, the assessment of the Pauline opinion changes, at times in diametrical fashion. Does Paul demand that Christian women abide by the common, everyday custom in worship while the women in Corinth wanted to emancipate themselves from this custom of wearing veils?[78] Or is Paul trying to impose on Greek women the more specifically Jewish custom of wearing veils?[79] Or does Paul want to persuade Christian women to enter the congregation according to everyday custom with their hair tied back (with or without bow) and no longer appear in worship with loose hair, as was common in pagan cultic custom?[80] When examining portraits of women from Greece and Rome, the picture remains manifold. Women without head cover are depicted next to women with head cover in the same context, and the marital status of the women does not offer a consistent explanation of the differing outfit.[81] One will have to assume that in the streets of Corinth, as elsewhere in the Roman Empire, women wore differently bound, long hairstyles with or without a himation pulled over the head, with or without mitra or ribbons. Presumably, city women of higher casts in the Near East already at that time veiled their faces—including Jewish women.[82]

The Pauline text, however, is not concerned with the wearing of a veil—that is, with a partial covering of the face; instead, it is concerned with the covering of the head by a himation, a cape, a mitra, and so on. This fact is made clear, on the one hand, by the terminology Paul uses, and, on the other, by the fact that texts that mean a veiling of the face will say so explicitly.[83] The actual divergence in everyday custom was met in Greek and Roman literature of the day with strongly expressed opinions in which the demand is raised that the honorable, free, and married woman express her honor by means of a head cover—and some women seem to have yielded to this demand.[84] It would seem that this conservative custom did not gain acceptance to the extent that a woman walking the street without head cover would have been considered dishonorable. Paul is not alone with his demand or, most likely, with his insight (1 Cor. 11:16) that this demand cannot be easily put into practice, for the actual custom of Rome and Greece appears much more diverse and free. By the way, among people in the country—and among the very poor—this whole issue will have hardly played a role.[85]

Why does Paul make this demand? Why do all churches known to him practice the custom he calls for (1 Cor. 11:16)? At the center of Pauline argumentation stands an interest in the visible demonstration of the woman's role in society, namely that she be subject to the man. The magical idea that through the woman's ties with the man the grasp of the angels becomes impossible (1 Cor. 11:10) plays only a minor role. Paul does not demand a proper outfit for the matron who walks in the city's streets, as does the strict husband in Valerius Maximus.[86] Instead, he makes this demand for the appearance of women in worship service. However, since specific problems play only a marginal role in relation to the cult, one can conclude from his argument on the woman's role in society that he is concerned with a social and public problem.

The worship service is viewed as a public event that nonmembers may attend (1 Cor. 14:23) and by which the church also expresses its social self-image. The next step in the argument's development relates to the public nature of the congregation: "Women should be silent in the churches" (1 Cor. 14:33b–36). Again this demand postulates the woman's submission to the man (see vv. 34ff.). Whether this demand comes from Paul himself or was added later to 1 Corinthians may remain open. At any rate, the development leading up to 1 Cor. 14:33b–36 had started already during Paul's time and in what he stated in 1 Cor. 11:2–16.

A consistent line runs from 1 Cor. 11:2–16 to 1 Tim. 2:11–15 and Titus 2:3–5 (and to Col. 3:18 and 1 Pet. 3:1–7; though Eph. 5:21–23 is part of this line, its portrayal of the relationship between man and woman is more sensitive and differentiated). The woman's submission is viewed in its public and social context. A Christian woman is supposed to win her non-Christian husband for the gospel without words, by her modest and pure life (1 Pet. 3:1–6). She is not supposed to teach but to submit and be blessed by having children (1 Tim. 2:1ff.). In my view, Titus 2:5 aptly expresses the point of these commands for Christian women: "so that the word of God may not be discredited." The worries about being discredited play a role elsewhere in the context of these instructions as, for example, in Titus 2:8, 10 and 1 Tim. 3:6ff. By and large, these instructions to women, as in general with early Christian instruction, are not addressing "problems" within the churches; this is true also for the pastoral letters, although Christian women are there harshly criticized for their independence (2 Tim. 3:6–7; 1 Tim. 5:3–16). As little as Paul is arguing in Rom. 13:1–7 against political dreamers and fanatics,[87] as little does he argue in 1 Cor. 11:2–16 against "exaggerated" emancipation.[88] He has the non-Christian public in mind. But the issue is not to adapt Christianity to the bourgeoisie of the day, neither for Paul nor the pastoral letters.[89] The general situation of the Christian community remains constant: Its members are politically endangered, experience heavy public pressure, and are mainly without rank, influence, or financial means. The discrediting that Titus 2:5 mentions has to be placed in the context of denunciations that led to state trials and, in some cases, also to the execution of Christians. See on that point Mark 13:11–13, for example, which describes prophesies that need to be read as descriptions of present sufferings in the Roman Empire.

In actual fact, the women in the churches enjoyed definite equality and partnership with the men in their work and role. Their role differed, hence, from the ideas of ruling figures in politics, administration, and culture. That role—like a number of other Christian practices—not only constituted a complete opposite to society's reality and ideology, but also caused suspicion in that society.[90] The latter point is underlined by the way Marcion reads Luke 23:2—Jesus is accused of having seduced women and children—and again by the repetition of this accusation by Celsus in Origen (see *Contra Celsum* 3.44).[91] The contradiction between the Christian practice of equality in New Testament times and the restrictive admonitions to Christian women by such men as Paul is understandable in light of the political and social situation of the Christian community. These admonitions are just as defensive as, for example, those in Rom. 13:1–7. One tries to keep points of offense small and to limit them to the crucial—namely, the confession of the God of Israel and of Christ the Messiah. It appears, however, that the actual loss of liberating practice that such a defensive attitude caused took place not until the second century. If one looks in the New Testament at the traces of reality in the congregations spoken of there, one is not left with the impression that the women were quiet in the church, not even in the churches to which the pastoral letters were addressed. And of all documents on the "emancipation" of Christian women, Luke-Acts is most emphatic, and it originates from the end of the first century. The role of women also in the Gospel of Mark (see above) presupposes an unrestricted partnership of women and men in the churches.

First Cor. 11:2–16 as well as the utterances concerning the role of women contained in those letters later attributed to Paul are documents of "male chauvinism." I have no doubt about that. However, "male chauvinism" can be quite varied in content. For a minority of people—under the political and social pressure of the Roman Empire and eager to survive the struggle to proclaim and practice their hope—the instruction for women in 1 Cor. 11:2–16 is a protective attitude at the expense of women, externally imposed. Leaving aside the heavy pressure, the contradictory situation of Christian women is grotesque almost from the beginning of the spread of Christianity in the Roman Empire (1 Cor. 11:16). Paul tells such things as 1 Cor. 11:3 to women who have equal rights in proclaiming the Christian message and who build churches, women such as Prisca or Phoebe. Further, women live in churches in which originate instructions concerning them like those in the pastoral letters, even though the work they do even after 70 C.E. is still being described in the manner in which the Gospels of Mark or Luke speak about women as disciples of Jesus. After all that is known about Christianity of the first century, women were certainly important bearers of the Christian faith (see only Romans 16 and the role of Mary Magdalene). One should only imagine the situation where a Christian man reads 1 Tim. 2:11–15 to those Christian women who, like the martyrs of Scili in Numidia (180 C.E.), stand their ground in a trial the same way as men do and are executed just the same.[92]

Luke

The Gospel of Luke differs from the other Christian literature of New Testament times insofar as one finds here the factual equality of women in the churches also reflected in thought so that the contradiction between practice and instruction is removed. Among the rich and well-respected Christians, whom Luke addresses in his Gospel, there are women who independently and actively take part in the Christian work.[93] Luke tells stories in which women—for instance, Tabitha or Lydia (Acts 9:36–40; 16:14–40)—play an exemplary role. Also, Prisca is an independently acting woman in Luke's opinion. In Acts 18:26, she is called the first of those who, together with her husband, teach Apollos proper doctrine. Luke is not afraid to speak of a "female disciple" (Acts 9:36) and of "prophetesses" (Acts 21:9; Luke 2:36). Even the story of Jesus' birth becomes in Luke a portrayal of exemplary women, Elizabeth and Mary. They are the mothers of John the Baptist and of Jesus, but their faith and their insight (1:25, 42, 45, 60; 2:19) make them representatives of the faith through whom people as disciples of Jesus can find guidance. They are role models not only for women.

In two little scenes (Luke 10:38–42 and 11:27–28), Luke[94] presents a vivid image of the problems resulting from the socially prescribed role of women for the women as disciples of Jesus. Mary and Martha are not depicted as individual people but as types that represent a role, a certain behavior. Mary represents the "hearing of the word" (see v. 39); she is the pupil sitting at Jesus' feet and listening to the teacher's words, whose words are the word of God.[95]

Martha represents the role of the woman in the house, the "serving" (*diakonein*) task in the sense of preparing meals and taking care of the house. Her behavior (she is "kept totally busy" by all the house work, v. 40) is to dramatize what the fate of most women is, except for the rich: She works in the house. As a rule, the woman working in the house is probably also working to earn money besides (see above). Housework is described here in quite realistic terms. Martha is not the ideal woman, "a house mother full of diligence and reliability,"[96] but a house mother full of diligence and strain and one to give vent to her irritation.

Mary represents a new woman's role in the context of early Christianity: the female disciple of Jesus, the woman who follows Jesus as his disciple, who could be compared at best in social-historical terms with the woman Hipparchia, who was a Kynic itinerant philosopher.[97] From what has been said so far, one can conclude that the women of early Christianity from Mary Magdalene to the female martyrs in Scili (see above) did in actual fact have an equal role in the work and proclamation of the churches. These are the ones spoken of in the person of Mary. While the Gospel of Mark, for example, is at great ease placing the two roles of women right next to each other,[98] the Gospel of Luke has reflected on this contrast quite deliberately.

The same issue appears in Luke 11:27–28. The beatitude of Mary as the mother of the Messiah is juxtaposed to Jesus' beatitude of those who hear and keep the word of God. Both scenes also interpret each other. The woman who in Luke 11:26 blesses Mary acts toward Mary, the mother of Jesus, the same way as Martha acts toward her sister Mary: She tries to restrict her in front of Jesus to her traditional woman's role. In contrast to the pastoral letters (or those of Paul), it is remarkable here that the voice advocating the traditional woman's role is placed into the mouths of women. Hence, it is here not a matter of Christian men who, feeling responsible for the fate of the congregations, impose on women a certain role—as in 1 Tim. 2:11–12—but it is a much more immediate situation: Women themselves have to be aware of the relationship of these two roles to each other and have probably often enough been forced to bear the reality of conflict between Martha and Mary. After all, Martha does not act out of malice toward Mary. Often, the conflict between Martha and Mary might, especially among the poorer women, become a conflict within the woman. One might try imagining this concrete situation, and one will understand how this conflict between Martha and Mary can occur.

Jesus' answer criticizes Martha, just as his answer in 11:28 criticizes the beatitude of Mary, which has reduced her to belly and breasts.

Jesus' critical answer says in 10:41-42: "Martha, Martha, you worry much and work hard. But only one thing is needed. Mary has chosen the good part, and it will not be taken away from her" [trans. from author's German].[99] The crucial question is: Is Martha humiliated by Jesus' reply, or is she even told that her conduct will lead to hell? When *agathē meris* is translated as a comparative, Martha's work is degraded: She has chosen the worse part. Let her be humiliated and go back to the kitchen! However, one has to interpret "the good part" in an eschatological fashion.[100] The "good part" Mary has chosen is eternal salvation. But does Jesus' answer not make things worse when it is given an eschatological content? Does Martha now have her part with the godless? From the story itself—but also from Luke 11:27-28—it is obvious that none of that is intended. As little as Jesus' mother, just because she is his mother, is degraded in the Gospel of Luke, as little is Martha's work to be degraded. The point is not to reduce the women as disciples of Jesus to the roles of housewife and mother. Mary is not played out against Martha in Luke 10:38-42. Jesus' answer would have been even more convincing for today's sensitivities if he had gone into the kitchen along with Mary, and before Martha complained, and if all three of them had prepared the meal.... But that is not the historic experience of early Christians. The good part Mary has chosen, Martha should choose also; that is Jesus' implied admonition. Jesus here defends women who are his disciples against forces that try to reduce women to the roles of housewives and mothers. Jesus expects that women will in actual fact bear a "double load." Martha will have to manage both—and this is also the way it might actually have been in the Christian homes of the first century: The women worked for God's word and took care of the housework (and worked in a job). In the houses of the rich Christians—as in Lydia's—it would have been the slaves who had to perform this double task. Certainly, the slaves were allowed to listen to the apostle Paul when he was visiting at Lydia's (Acts 16:15). However, they had to do their jobs also. For today's ideas on the role of women (or even today's ideas on slavery), the solution presented in the Gospel of Luke might appear insufficient. Nevertheless, a very important step has been taken, in my view, when women are no longer reduced to such a role.

The ancient church viewed Luke 10:38–42 in a symbolic sense: Martha represents the *vita activa* and Mary the *vita contemplativa*.[101] Modern interpretation also does not perceive this narrative as a problem of women's roles; it says, for example, that this story "teaches the only valuable aspiration."[102] Such interpretations emerge when, in the interpretation of the narrative, Martha is forgotten; when Mary is isolated from Martha; or when one lacks insight on the reality of the kind of conflict described here and can grasp it only as a symbol for something else. In the context of the Gospel of Luke and in the context of the story about the women as disciples of Jesus, this story—just as Luke 11:27–28—is a reflection of the roles of women. Many symbolic, spiritualized, and allegorical interpretations of biblical traditions have removed the biblical concreteness, and the transtemporal generalization, gained thus, has robbed people of their history. By means of a spiritualized interpretation concerning the beatitude of the poor, interpreters have obscured the fact that we owe the poor Jews of Palestine of the first century the hope we receive from the Gospels. By means of a symbolic and generalizing interpretation of Mary and Martha, interpreters have pushed into utter oblivion the fact that many women were part of the proclamation of the gospel—not individual, outstanding, "great" women, but the many women who were among the most destitute of Palestine, as well as the many women in the churches that knew Paul and Luke. After all, the story of Mary and Martha does not address the problems of individual great women but the everyday problems of women among the little people, who entered discipleship of Jesus through their practice.

Notes

1. On the factual autonomy concerning property rights in the Roman Empire, see M. Kaser, *Das römische Privatrecht*, HAW 10, 3.3.1 (Munich, 1971), 329; for those rights in the Greece of the classical and Hellenistic times, see K. Thraede, "Frau," *RAC* 8 (1970): 199, and idem, "Ärger mit der Freiheit," in G. Scharffenorth and K. Thraede, *Freunde in Christus werden...* (Gelnhausen, 1977), 46–47. One will have to ask whether upper-class Jewish families in Palestine and the provinces kept Jewish laws rather than Roman-Hellenistic ones, since such adherence has been documented in relation to divorces; see Josephus, *Ant.* 15.259; 18.136; perhaps also *Vita* 415.

2. See R. Etienne, *Pompeji: Das Leben in einer antiken Stadt* (Frankfurt, n.d.), 169–72 (cf. the Stuttgart edition, 1974).

3. See Egyptian documents from the national museums in Berlin, *Griechische Urkunden IV* (Berlin, 1912), no. 1116; German translation H. Thierfelder, *Unbekannte antike Welt* (Gütersloh, 1963), 72–73; see also H. Metzger, *Nachrichten aus dem Wüstensand* (Zurich, 1974), 29–30.

4. *Sammelbuch griechischer Urkunden aus Ägypten* (Wiesbaden, 1971), 10:10532; see also text and translation in J. Hengstl, ed., *Griechische Papyri aus Ägypten als Zeugnisse des öffentlichen und privaten Lebens* (Munich, 1978), 357–58; for further documents, see Papyrus Warren 12 in above collection, 360–61, or, for example, H. Dessau, *Inscriptiones Latinae Selectae* (Berlin, 1955), 2/1:7370. Here, a *domina* landlord erects a tombstone for her caretaker.

5. V. A. Tcherikover and A. Fuks, eds., *Corpus Papyrorum Judaicarum I* (Jerusalem: Magnes Press, 1957), no. 28Z, 25ff.; no. 47; no. 41.

6. Suetonius, *Claudius* 18ff.; for more material on business activities of women, see Thraede, "Frau," 204, 223; idem, in Scharffenorth and Thraede, *Freunde*, 46, 78. See also L. Huchthausen, "Zu kaiserlichen Reskripten an weibliche Adressaten aus der Zeit Diokletians," *Klio* 58 (1976): 55–86.

7. On Poppaea Sabina, see especially Suetonius, *Nero* 35; *Otho* 3; Tacitus, *Ann.* 13.45ff.; 14.64. See also D. Balsdon, *Die Frau in der römischen Antike* (Munich, 1979), 137ff.

8. Ovid, *Ars amatoria* 239ff.; German translation from P. *Ovidius Naso, Liebeskunst, Lateinisch-deutsch* (Munich, 1969). Juvenal's contentions concerning women's hunger for power and the arbitrariness with which they had slaves crucified may be spiteful but certainly not completely invented (Juvenal, Satire 6.219ff.).

9. Such is the title of an essay by M. J. Finley, "The Silent Women of Rome," *Horizon* 7 (1965): 57–64.

10. See the respective speeches of hatred by Juvenal, Satire 6.434ff.

11. See especially Juvenal, Satire 6.595ff. (cf. also 6.360ff.). One has to take into account, however, that birth control and abortion are not always clearly distinguished, and that contraceptives, discussed in the medical literature of antiquity, are only partially effective; likewise, this literature does not distinguish between contraceptives and means effecting sterility. For a comprehensive discussion of the matter, see K. Hopkins, "Contraception in the Roman Empire," *Comparative Studies in Society and History* (1965): 124–51.

12. For an example, see the sixth satire of Juvenal. Further material has been gathered by L. Friedländer, *Darstellungen aus der Sittengeschichte Roms*, 10th ed. (Leipzig, 1922), 1:283–84.

13. See Stobäus, ed. C. Wachsmuth and O. Hense, 2d ed. (Berlin, 1958), 2:238, esp. line 9; 244, esp. lines 19–20; German trans. in *Epiktet, Teles und Musonius*, trans. W. Capelle (Zurich, 1948).

14. Valerius Maximus, *Factorum Dictorumque Memorabilium Libri Novem* 8.3.2.

15. Ibid., 2.1.3. Concerning the ideal of the *univira*, see Thraede, "Frau," 218.

16. Valerius Maximus, *Factorum* 4.4.

17. Ibid., 2.1.2. For more information on this "conservative nest ideology" (Thraede) of the Roman upper class, see

Thraede, "Frau," 215; idem, in Scharffenorth and Thraede, *Freunde*, 79ff.; Balsdon, *Die Frau*, 229.

18. Thraede, "Frau"; idem, in Scharffenorth and Thraede, *Freunde*.

19. Plutarch, *Coniugalia praecepta* (Mor. 138Aff.), esp. 140A and 140D; German translation in *Plutarch: Von der Ruhe des Gemütes und andere philosophische Schriften*, Bibliothek der Alten Welt (Zurich, 1948), 93ff.

20. For an example, see Juvenal, Satire 6.526ff. For more material, see Friedländer, *Darstellungen*, 1:302ff. and S. K. Heyob, *The Cult of Isis Among Women in the Graeco-Roman World* (Leiden: E. J. Brill, 1975). For women who had a religion different from their husbands, see for example Tertullian, *Apologeticum* 15; 1 Corinthians 7; Josephus, *BJ* 2.560–61.

21. See Thraede, in Scharffenorth and Thraede, *Freunde*, 79ff.; R. I. Frank, "Augustus' Legislation on Marriage and Children," *California Studies in Classical Antiquity* 8 (1975): 41–52.

22. Valerius Maximus, *Factorum* 3.8.6; cf. 8.8. Such a performance can be imagined only as a heroic exception; see 8.3.3.

23. Thus, it can be concluded from Ovid, *Tristia* 2.207ff.

24. In *Tristia* 2.239ff., Ovid defends himself before the emperor by referring to *Ars amatoria* 1.31–34. He says that his work did not break legal orders. He contends that he tried to keep out of his writing all those women who could not be touched due to their wearing veils and trains. W. Stroh, "Ovids Liebeskunst und die Ehegesetze des Augustus," *Gymnasium* 86 (1979): 323–52, shows the connection between the *Ars amatoria* and the emperor's marital laws. On the one hand, Ovid secures himself; on the other, he mocks the marital laws.

25. See Dio Cassius, 54.15.5; see also Macrobius, *Saturnalia* 2.5.6. Livia appears in public surrounded by a protective group of older men—in contrast to her step-daughter Julia, who is accompanied by young and elegant people. See also Tacitus on this matter (*Ann.* 5.1.5).

26. See especially Suetonius, *Augustus* 62; Tacitus, *Ann.* note 5.1.

27. Dio Cassius, 54.16.5.

28. Tacitus, *Ann.* 13.45ff.

29. See the analysis of Livius, 34.2–8, in Thraede's article in Scharffenorth and Thraede, *Freunde*, 82–83. See esp. Livius,

34.2.4 and 34.5.5. See also Augustus's speech in Dio Cassius, 56.1–10 (on the role of the woman 56.3.3).

30. German text and translation, *Römische Grabinschriften,* ed. G. Pfohl, trans. H. Geist (Munich, 1969), no. 22 (=Dessau 8444).

31. Xenophon, *Oeconomicus* 7ff.; 12ff. German trans., *Xenophons "Oikonomikos,"* trans. K. Meyer (Marburg, 1975).

32. Columella, *De re rustica* 12, preface; German trans., *Über die Landwirtschaft,* trans. K. Ahrens (Berlin, 1976).

33. Ibid., 12.3.6.

34. Antipater of Tarsus, in Stobäus, ed. Wachsmuth and Hense, 4:509, lines 12ff.

35. Pliny the Younger, *Epistulae* 10.96.7ff.; see also A. Wlosok, *Rom und die Christen* (Stuttgart, 1970), 32–33. The listing of crimes not committed by (former) Christians has not been defined by Christians—as through the Decalogue, for example: "not committing thefts, robberies (*latrocinia*), adulteries; not offending loyalty and faith (*fidem fallere*); not giving false witness." The political connection is clearest for *latrocinium,* for armed upheaval. See on that M. Hengel, *Die Zeloten* (Leiden, 1976), 24ff. On the interpretation of the text, see A. N. Sherwin-White, *The Letters of Pliny* (Oxford: Oxford University Press, 1966), 706–7; R. Freudenberger, *Das Verhalten der römischen Behörden gegen die Christen im 2. Jahrhundert* (Munich, 1967), 168–69, concludes from the nonpolitical attitude of Christians, however, that here the political aspect moves in the background.

36. Athenagoras, Sup. 31.

37. Diodorus Siculus, 3.13.1–3. Christian women, too, were later condemned to work in mines; see F. Augar, *Die Frau im römischen Christenprozess,* Texte und Untersuchungen, 13/4 (1905), 78.

38. Columella, *De re rustica* 12.3.6; for the interpretation as presented here, see H. Gummerus, *Der römische Gutsbetrieb* (Leipzig, 1906), 89–90.

39. Columella, *De re rustica* 12, preface, 4–5.

40. See also the more or less accidental mentioning of children of the *pauperculi* in farm work in Varro, *De re rustica* 1.17.

41. *Martyrium Pionii,* 9.4 (selected acts of martyrs; newly edited in the Knopf edition by B. Krüger, with an addendum

by G. Ruhrbach, 4th ed. [Tübingen, 1965], 50). The former slave Sabina is tied up by the woman who had released her earlier and sent into the mountains to deter her from her Christian faith; that is, she was probably sent to a farm in an *ergastulum*. On this interpretation, see J. Scheele, "Zur Rolle der Unfreien in den römischen Christenverfolgungen" (Diss., University of Tübingen, 1970), 63.

42. All these words come from Pollux, *Onomasticon* 1.222; 7.141–42, 150. Further material in P. Herfst, *Le travail de la femme dans la Grèce ancienne* (Utrecht, 1922), 15–17, whose judgment that the role of the woman in farming was not important is caused by the above-mentioned problems of sources; even his own source material reveals that his judgment is incorrect.

43. See Mishna *Baba Mesi'a* 7:6; see also S. Krauss, *Talmudische Archäologie* (Leipzig, 1911), 2:46.

44. I am only pointing in general to J. Le Gall, "Métiers de femmes au Corpus Inscriptionum Latinarum," in *Revue des Études Latines*, Mélanges Marcel Durry (1969), 47:123–30. See also easily accessible material, such as *Römische Grabinschriften*, nos. 130, 132, 174, 175, 195, 207, 248, 251, 252, 253, 259, 275–80, 292, 358, 361, 377, 378, 385.

45. See on that S. Treggiari, "Jobs for Women," *American Journal of Ancient History* 1 (1976): 76–104. Plautus draws a very concrete caricature of the female staff of rich women in Plautus, *Miles gloriosus* 678–722 and in *Trinummus* 252–54.

46. *Papiri greci e latini*, 4:599; German trans., H. Thierfelder, *Unbekannte antike Welt* (Gütersloh, 1963), 71; on the interpretation, see S. Thierfelder, "Zur sozialen Lage der Weber in Ägypten," *Zeitschrift für Geschichtswissenschaft* 5 (1957): 118–23.

47. *Der Maximaltarif bei Diocletian*, annotated by H. Blümner (Berlin, 1893), 20.12; 20.13; 21.6; German trans., K. Bücher, *Beiträge zur Wirtschaftsgeschichte* (Tübingen, 1922), 228ff.

48. Bücher, *Beiträge*, 217.

49. One example is Pap. Rylands 2.167 (Egypt, 39 C.E.); text and translation in Hengstl, ed., *Griechische Papyri*, no. 148.

50. There is, to my knowledge, no reason to assume that Prisca and Aquila were a wealthy and sophisticated "business couple" (Thraede, in Scharffenorth and Thraede, *Freunde*, 97). The most likely assumption is, in my view, that Paul, Aquila, and Prisca made blankets for Roman military tents. In Acts 18:3, the version of the Codex Sinaiticus and others (*ērgazonto*)

is to be preferred. The singular in the Western text is part of the unambiguous and later attempts to conceal Prisca's role; see on that A. von Harnack, "Über die beiden Recensionen der Geschichte der Prisca und des Aquila in Act. Apost. 18, 1–12," in *Sitzungsberichte der Königlich-Preussischen Akademie der Wiss. zu Berlin* (1900), 1/2. Acts 18:3 says that Paul stayed "with them" (i.e., with Prisca and Aquila) and that they (not only Paul and Aquila, but all three of them) worked together in their profession (differently in W. Michaelis, *TWNT* 7:395).

51. See on that W. Stegemann, in L. Schottroff and W. Stegemann, *Jesus and the Hope of the Poor* (Maryknoll, N.Y.: Orbis Books, 1986), 82–87.

52. Only the woman who anoints Jesus with perfume in the house of Simon might be considered one of the wealthy women who already in Palestine had become sympathetic to the Jesus movement (Mark 14:3–9). She certainly is well-to-do if she can afford to spend three hundred denarii on perfume oil. But for Luke she was a prostitute (Luke 7:36–50). It is unlikely that this story is indeed part of the Jesus movement in Palestine on account of how it speaks of the poor: as objects of almsgiving; on top of that, the almsgiving is relativized (Mark 14:7). The story's view of the social conditions at the time matches the view of Mark's story: The Christians of Mark's faith communities are not *ptōchoi*, destitute, but still know wealth only from a distance. Concerning expensive perfume oil they think only of how to turn it into money. It is the same view as Mark 10:17–31. These texts belong in a different situation than those concerning the beatitudes of the poor and the rejoicing over the eschatological miracles done on the crippled and the poor (Matt. 11:2–5 par.; Luke 6:20–21).

53. For the methodological steps presupposed here for the reconstruction of older traditions, see L. Schottroff, in Schottroff and Stegemann, *Jesus*, 1ff., 38–39.

54. See on that ibid., 46.

55. Even though Luke 16:18 goes back to Q in its wording, it cannot refer to inner-community problems of divorce, given the way Q is shaped by the announcement of judgment; it is more likely that this text refers to a particular practice of divorces followed by remarriage outside the community. I owe this thesis to P. Nickel.

56. This fact can be deduced from Philo, *De Specialibus Legibus* 3.158ff. In the Codex Hammurabi one finds a rule that disputes the claim of the fugitive for his deserted wife, in case she has entered another marriage; see W. Eilers, *Die Gesetzesstele des Chammurabis* (Leipzig, 1936), par. 136.

57. See on that L. Schottroff, in Schottroff and Stegemann, *Jesus*, 15–16.

58. See on that L. Swidler, *Women in Judaism* (Metuchen, N.J.: Scarecrow Press, 1976), 130–39.

59. The text itself does not give the reason for her caution. The idea of uncleanliness resulting from touch is held by Billerbeck, 1:520, and R. Hengel and M. Hengel, "Die Heilungen Jesu und medizinisches Denken," in *Medicus Viator* (Tübingen, 1959), 338–39. The other thesis, that the woman felt shame because of her disease, is held by E. Klostermann, *Das Markusevangelium*, HNT 3, 4th ed. (Tübingen, 1950), on that particular passage.

60. Pliny the Elder, *Naturalis historia* 7.64; 28.23.

61. There, one could acquire quite solid and enlightened insights on menstruation and women's diseases. The therapeutic possibilities that Soranus (second century C.E.), for example, recommends in his book on gynecology (chap. 11) for someone letting blood are probably out of the question for the woman of Mark 5:25ff. due to financial reasons. The doctors, who took the woman's money (certainly no great amount of it), are hardly as educated as those in Alexandria and were not likely inclined to try such a specific therapy, connected with a vast amount of care.

62. See the discussion on that passage in R. Pesch, *Das Markusevangelium* (Freiburg, 1977), vol. 2.

63. On the meaning of *diakonia*, see the term *diakonos Christou* or *theou* (2 Cor. 6:4; 11:23) and the material and the arguments by D. Georgi, *Die Gegner des Paulus im 2. Korintherbrief* (Neukirchen, 1964), 32–38.

64. See the history of the text of Acts 17:4, 12 and the role of Prisca in Acts 18:1ff.; see note 50.

65. M. Hengel, "Maria Magdalena und die Frauen als Zeugen," in *Abraham unser Vater* (Leiden, 1963), 243–56, esp. 253, where he correctly sees this same connection (different from R. Pesch, *Das Markusevangelium*, 2:536), yet views it as pre-Markan. In my view, one needs to agree with his thesis

that Mary Magdalene was "the first to bring the disciples the message of the Lord's resurrection" (see p. 256).

66. See mainly Billerbeck, 3:560; M. Hengel, "Maria," 246.

67. The defamation of Christians because of the role of women in their communities and, in particular, their role in the Easter proclamation is not based on such specific Jewish or legal aspects. See mainly Celsus in Origen, *Contra Celsum* 2.55, and Luke 23:2 in Marcion's text (the charges against Jesus are expanded by saying that he makes both women and children obstinate). See also n. 91, below.

68. See W. Bousset, *Kyrios Christos*, 5th ed. (Göttingen, 1965), 65; R. Bultmann, *Die Geschichte der synoptischen Tradition*, 4th ed. (Göttingen, 1958), 308. Reports of appearances of Jesus such as 1 Cor. 15:3–8 or a report like Mark 16:1–8 seem to me not too divergent theologically, historically, or in terms of *Formgeschichte*. Even in Mark 16:1–8 the issue is the command to tell the message of the resurrection.

69. See on that L. Schottroff, "Das Magnificat und die älteste Tradition über Jesus von Nazareth," in *EvT* 38 (1978): 298ff.; Schottroff and Stegemann, *Jesus*, 28–29.

70. '*Abot* 2:7 and 1:5 (cf. Sir. 9:9); see for example J. Leipoldt, *Die Frau in der antiken Welt und im Urchristentum*, 3d ed. (Leipzig, 1965), 62, 67; or A. Oepke, *TWNT* 1:782. See also n. 97, below, on these questions.

71. Thraede, "Frau," 224–25.

72. On this differentiation, see especially E. Schüssler Fiorenza, "Women in the Pre-Pauline and Pauline Churches," *USQR* 33 (1978): 153–66. On Gal. 3:28, see especially H. Thyen, in F. Crüsemann and H. Thyen, *Als Mann und Frau geschaffen* (Gelnhausen, 1978), 107ff.

73. Especially G. Theissen has examined this question in detail (see G. Theissen, *Studien zur Soziologie des Urchristentums* [Tübingen, 1979], 201ff.). He arrives at the conclusion, however, that the Pauline communities were socially mixed. The discussion of Theissen's argument cannot be presented here in detail. As Theissen shows, the socioeconomic characteristics of persons (like the "city treasurer" [Rom. 16:23]) remain ambiguous throughout. Is Phoebe (Rom. 16:1–2) a well-to-do benefactress of Lydia's kind (Acts 16:11ff.), or is she, although owning a home that she offers to Paul and the community, still far from wealthy? Also, the reason for the journey remains

ambiguous; it could be a move in search of better working conditions as is the case for Aquila and Prisca (see n. 50, above). The decisive argument appears to be 2 Corinthians 8. There is an economic gap between Corinth and the communities in Macedonia. The richer Corinthian congregation could not refuse to take part in the collection for the destitute of Jerusalem by claiming that by doing so, it would put itself in hardship, although it was itself not well off (8:13).

74. Concerning the proper names, see H. Lietzmann, *An die Römer,* HNT 8, 3d ed. (Tübingen, 1928) on that passage.

75. See B. Brooten, "Junia... Outstanding Among the Apostles (Romans 16:7)," in L. Swidler and A. Swidler, eds., *Women Priests* (New York: Paulist Press, 1977), 141–44.

76. On the meaning of *prostatis,* see mainly H. Schaefer, PW Sup 9 (1962), 1302–3.

77. It makes no sense that the use of *kephalē* is not supposed to express a relationship from above to below in the sense of superiority and power. Paul probably does not rely on the explicitly metaphorical use of *kephalē,* but he plays with the concrete meaning of the word (head), on the one hand (as, for example, the double meaning of the word in v. 5 where *kephalē* can mean the head of the man or the woman), and the rank of the head versus the body, on the other. Repeatedly, Paul emphasizes the superiority of the man and the inequality between man and woman: She is made "out of" him, but he *not* of her (v. 8; see vv. 5, 9, 14–15). The relationship indicated by *kephalē* cannot be reversed. R. Scroggs argues differently. For him, *kephalē* means "source" in the metaphorical sense, and 1 Cor. 11:3 is a midrash on Genesis 2, which does not contend male superiority (see especially R. Scroggs, "Paul and the Eschatological Woman: Revisited," *JAAR* 42 [1974]: 534–35).

78. This interpretation is advanced, though cautiously, by H. Conzelmann, *Der erste Brief an die Korinther,* 11th ed. (Göttingen, 1969), 218.

79. A. Oepke, *TWNT* 3:564.

80. See, e.g., S. Lösch, "Christliche Frauen in Korinth," *TQ* 127 (1974): 216–61.

81. See the Ara Pacis; and especially on this question, H. Brandenburg, *Studien zur Mitra* (Münster, 1966), esp. 102–8; H. Blanck, *Einführung in das Privatleben der Griechen und Römer* (Darmstadt, 1976), 60ff.; for our question especially helpful is

A. Rüsch, "Das kaiserzeitliche Porträt in Mazedonien," in *Jahrbuch des Deutschen Archäologischen Instituts* 84 (1969): 59–196; on tombstones, wives are depicted wearing himations pulled over their heads, but there are also wives without head covers.

82. This question is debated; see on that S. Krauss, *Talmudische Archäologie* (Leipzig, 1910), 1:189 (no veiling of Jewish women); E. Marmorstein, "The Veil in Judaism and Islam," *JJS* 5 (1954): 1–11 (the Jewish woman in the city wears a veil).

83. A veiling of the face is described, for example, in Dio Chrysostom, 33.48. Paul speaks of covering the *head* or the absence of the head cover in verses 4, 5, 6, 7, 10, 13; also verse 15; *peribolaion* means cape, not veil.

84. Valerius Maximus (*Factorum* 6.3.10) speaks of the hardness of C. Sulpicius Gallus, who dismissed his wife because she was seen with uncovered head in public, and he declares: "A harsh judgment, which, nevertheless, does not lack good reason." Concerning the procedure against women suspected of adultery according to Num. 5:18, Philo says (*De Specialibus Legibus* 3.56), contrary to that Old Testament text (and also to Num. 5:18 in the Septuagint), that in this legal case the priest removes the head cover (*epikranon*) from the woman "so that she be judged with her head exposed, bereft of the symbol of her shame which the absolutely chaste women usually use." In the same context, Josephus says that the priest pulls off the himation from the woman's head. The passage from Plutarch (*Quaestiones Romanae* 14), often cited in relation to 1 Corinthians 11, does not say either that, according to Roman tradition, women *indeed* covered their heads in public (see especially the comparative *synēthesteron* and the whole train of thought in context). Plutarch knows this Roman "custom" presumably as a demand. Hence, in Rome and the Roman Empire of this time in general, it was a conservative ideal of women, which expresses itself in the demand of morality-oriented men such as Valerius Maximus or Augustus and in the practice of certain women—those paying particular attention to demonstrating their honor. On Augustus, see Dio Cassius, 54.15.5, although there is no particular talk of the head cover. See also Ovid, *Ars amatoria* 1.30ff. Also the wearing of a veil was probably used as an expression of strict custom; see on that Tacitus, *Ann.* 13.45ff., and Dio Chrysostom, 33.48. The head cover of women and daughters of a free citizen on the street is, by

the way, already demanded in the Middle Assyrian legal code; see R. Haase, *Die keilschriftlichen Rechtssammlungen in deutscher Übersetzung* (Wiesbaden, 1963), 104, sec. 40.

85. One need not consider here the difference between the free and those set free or between the free and the nonfree. Although women set free are not subject to the same legal and moral demands as the free matron, there seems to be no massive difference between the actual outfits worn by the free and those set free (except for the difference based on different levels of wealth). E. von Dobschütz views libertines as "emancipated womenfolk," who within the Corinthian church are the "soul of opposition against the apostle and his rigorous discipline" (E. von Dobschütz, *Die urchristlichen Gemeinden* [Leipzig, 1902], 34–35). The situation of those set free, however, is characterized less by emancipation in this sense than by the fact that they slip more easily into the grey area of semiprostitution; see Stroh, "Ovids," 325–26, 335–36.

86. See n. 84, above.

87. See on that L. Schottroff, *Befreiungserfahrungen: Studien zur Sozialgeschichte des Neuen Testaments* (Munich, 1990), 57ff.

88. A common opinion; see A. von Harnack, *Die Mission und Ausbreitung des Christentums* (Leipzig, 1924), 2, 596; he assumes "strong excesses" on the women's part. What should these have been, though?

89. See M. Dibelius, *Die Pastoralbriefe*, HNT 13, 3d ed., ed. H. Conzelmann (Tübingen, 1955), on Titus 2:5; he speaks of a "typical agenda for the 'Christian bourgeois approach.'"

90. See on that nn. 35 and 36, above.

91. See also Porphyry's accusation against Christians for allowing women to hold power (see Harnack, *Die Mission*, 599); again see n. 67, above.

92. Three men and three women are tried and executed: see the Acta Scilitanorum in A. Wlosok, *Rom und die Christen* (Stuttgart, 1970).

93. See on that nn. 52 and 73, above. Luke is under the impression that already Jesus and Paul had won rich women for the gospel, which is probably historically incorrect. Only later, around the turn of the first century, did rich people begin to play a role in the churches, as Luke himself says, but see also the epistle of James.

94. "Luke" means here methodologically the following: In the literary context of the Gospel of Luke, the text has a certain meaning, which is dealt with here. But the question remains whether Luke is the "author" of this story. Even as a pre-Lukan isolated piece, its meaning would not change.

95. The theme of listening to Jesus' words (hence, to God's word) is important in the Gospel of Luke; to see how important, contrast Luke 8:21 to Mark.

96. From a Roman tombstone inscription; see n. 30, above.

97. See Diogenes Laertius, 6.96ff. In spite of the sociohistorical singularity of the role of the women as disciples of Jesus, one should not play Luke 10:38–42 against the behavior of a Jewish rabbi who thinks that women should not be instructed in the Torah (*Sota* 3:4); for example, W. Grundmann (*Das Evangelium nach Lukas*, THKNT 3 [Berlin, n.d.]) contrasts Luke 10:38–42 and Luke 8:2 on the basis of this Mishna passage. However, besides this passage there is also a contrasting one in *Sota* 3:4: "One is obliged to teach one's daughter the Torah." See also n. 70, above.

98. See nn. 62–63, above, on Mark 1:31 and 15:40–41.

99. From this kind of reading of one version of the handwritten traditions of the text (p^{45}, p^{75}, and other manuscripts), the development of all others can be explained best. The unease in the tradition of the text is caused by ascetic interests of the ancient church, which wanted to read here that Jesus recommends not to overdo things when it comes to eating.

100. *Agathē meris* is not the better part (as, for example, in W. Bauer, *Wörterbuch*), but the good part, the share in the kingdom of God. The idea of an eschatological *meros* speaks for this eschatological interpretation, as in Rev. 21:8; 22:19; Luke 12:46 par.; but esp. Luke 11:28 (*makarioi*).

101. On that and on other symbolic interpretations, see the respective commentaries.

102. So R. Bultmann, *Die Geschichte der synoptischen Tradition*, 4th ed. (Göttingen, 1958), 59. See also M. Dibelius, *Die Formgeschichte des Evangeliums*, 3d ed. (Tübingen, 1959), 116; all of it is simply dominated by the interest in Mary and the proclamation addressed to her.

5

Lydia:
A New Quality of Power

> *We went ... to Philippi, a city in the first district of Macedonia, a colony.... And on the Sabbath, we went outside the gate to the river, where we believed there was a place of worship, and we sat down and talked to the women gathered there. And one by the name of Lydia, a seller of purple fabrics from the city of Thyatira, a God-fearing woman, listened to us. God opened her heart so that she was attentive to what Paul was saying. After she and her household had been baptized, she asked: "When you are convinced that I believe in the Lord, come into my house and stay." And she compelled us. (Acts 16:12–15; see also 16:40) [trans. from author's German]*

    Lydia is originally from Thyatira in Asia Minor, a region heavily involved in the manufacturing and export of wool. All colors were called purple that resembled the original purple, yielded by the muricid mollusk. Since Lydia's home region had water that was particularly conducive for the dyeing of wool with plant colors, the dyed wool of this area was famous all over the Roman Empire. One needed for dyeing also other ingredients, frequently urine. At any rate, the dye-houses were, just like the tanneries, smelly places. One tried to place them outside the city, keeping in mind the main direction of the wind. In general, the manufacturing and the sale of dyed products were done by the same people. That means the dye-house was operated by an owner with several employees. These employees both worked in the dye-house and sold the wool. In the Latin language's treatment of those who worked with purple dye, no distinction is made between the male or female dyer and the male or female salesperson (both are called *purpurarius* or *purpuraria*), simply because both types of work were done by the same people. The profession was despised due to the bad smell connected with it. In addition, it was typically a women's profession. Since textile production had been women's work, done at home in preindustrialized ages, it remained women's work when textiles were produced outside the home in factories.

Lydia does not have a proper name, and that means she came from a socially unimportant family. Her name denotes her place of origin: "the one from Lydia." Such names, related to the place of origin, were often used for female and male slaves. Although Lydia is not a slave, her "name" points to the social irrelevance of her family. Lydia was a single woman. In early Christianity, we frequently encounter single women such as her, for example, Mary Magdalene and Tabitha. The Christian communities did not perceive such women as "somehow defective," since the text does not offer a hint of speculation in Lydia's case that she was a widow—as Christian interpreters often felt compelled to speculate. Early Christianity did not view marriage as the only way of God's will. The great number of single women in the Christian communities indicates that these women were received better here than they were used to being received elsewhere. We do not know what caused Lydia to come to Philippi in Macedonia all the way from Thyatira in Asia Minor. It must have had to do with her work. Many people in the Roman Empire traveled toward work places, just as did the tent makers Paul, Prisca, and Aquila.

At some point, Lydia came in contact with a Jewish synagogue community and started to live according to the Jewish religion. At any rate, by the river in Philippi she prayed to the God of Israel. Together with other Jewish women she formed an autonomous Jewish group of women. There are extrabiblical sources that document the existence of groups of women that accepted the Jewish religion on their own accord and practiced it as women's groups without male leadership or any other form of legitimization. In Philippi, Lydia heard the message that declared that Jesus was the Messiah, that he had died and risen, and that God was coming soon. God had opened her heart to this message. Her household was baptized. This "household" may have comprised relatives and male and female slaves. Even the lowly could, under certain circumstances, have a female slave. Her house, then, became the gathering place of the first Christian community in Philippi. We also know of other women, Prisca for example, who made their house the center of the new community of faith. In this house, one preached, shared meals, jointly administered the members' money, and organized one's everyday life according to the will of God. In this house, itinerant evangelists from out of town could stay, such as Paul, and explain their message without being expelled as strangers by the city officials; after all, the hostess vouched for the strangers before the city officials. This role of hostess must have been risky since, not without cause, Acts describes the political conflicts of these itinerant evangelists at great length. It took courage to be the hostess of such a new community and to these male and female itinerant evangelists (see Acts 17:7–9). In Philippi, the Christian itinerant evangelists were charged with hurting the business of the owner of a prophesying female slave (Acts 16:16–39). The house of a purple fabrics seller had become the Christian center of Philippi, just as the house of a tanner in Joppa (Acts 9:43; 10:6). The first male and female Christians were consistent in their practice of Jesus' message: "The last will be the first."

The exegetical history of the theology that is dominant to this day in the first world declares Lydia a well-to-do woman (and widow) who deals with luxury merchandise. Her praying together with other women has called forth a long discussion that insisted that the place of worship could not have been a synagogue and the women's worship service could not have been "proper." One can verify this exegetical history by opening any commentary on Acts. This exegetical history does not try to hide its intentions: The first female Christians had to be from the upper middle class; they were not allowed to question the patriarchal family and the patriarchal organization of religion. The fact that women work, and under very hard conditions at that, is rendered invisible. Also, no one takes time to ask what a woman does who sells purple fabrics. This exegetical history is so powerful that I myself believed for long what it said and had to take the laborious road of social-historical reconstruction in order to understand how especially women's work is rendered invisible. Future men and women readers of the Bible do not have to take the laborious road I took, if they ask these questions of the texts: What kind of work are the women doing? What can we find out about their living conditions? Yet people might object, saying: What does that have to do with theology? I think the question about the work of all people, and mainly of women, is very much a theological question, since it reveals what Christian faith has to do with everyday reality. In spite of their brevity, the sources we have are very rich in what they have to say, as Lydia's example shows. In a few words, the text says a great deal about Lydia.

Each detail of the story speaks of Lydia's power. She has gained power from her relationship with the God of Israel—at first, without knowing the message of Jesus' being the Messiah, later as a Christian. Her living conditions were miserable; her social reputation was extremely small. Perhaps, the other women by the river were in a similar situation. By the power she found in her relationship with the God of Israel, Lydia had built centers of solidarity: the community of a women's group living the Jewish faith and, in continuation of this community, a Christian house church. She "compelled" Paul and other men to be her guests. She took initiative to such an extent that even our source—Acts—briefly cites her speech, although our sources do not usually mention the speech of women. Lydia's speech calls for solidarity and community as a consequence of her faith. Paul and the other men were less interested in this consequence—at least in this case—than Lydia was. She insisted on having a house church in her home, knowing well that she thereby became conspicuous in the city and could possibly be persecuted for it.

In this story, it is especially important to me to recognize the intimate connection between the power, resulting from the relationship to the God of Israel, and the community. Lydia has brought people together and helped shape their common life anew. Searching for the history of women, of leading women, can be done from different perspectives. We can ask about the leadership of women and mean by "leadership" what we know of it from existing social institutions—especially from the church. This kind of leadership is a more or less veiled male power-hierarchy that no longer makes even men all too happy. Or, from another perspective, we can look at "leadership" in women's history or in the history of leading women by the example of Lydia's story. Her leadership arose when she brought people together into a community that was first oriented on the God of Israel and then on Jesus. This community perceived itself as a mustard seed of the coming kingdom of God. The power growing in this community was not the kind that makes others small but a power that is shared and wants to make others great when they are small and in misery. Lydia's "compelling" was an expression of a power not directed toward rule but toward justice.

The other quality of Lydia's power, which is not leadership in the hierarchical sense, can be illustrated by the parable of the mustard seed. The parable of the mustard seed concludes with a metaphor on political world power: the world tree, under whose branches are perching the birds of the sky. It was a picture for the great king at large or for the emperor, under whose "patronage" all nations are living in a state of submission and "peace," the peace of submission that is. The parable uses this picture to illustrate the "rule" of God as a king over all nations. With this parable it becomes clear that kings are no longer ruling over the nations but God. This royal rule of God, which puts an end to all human rule, is not of the same kind or quality as the rule of people over people. In the parable, the rule does not begin as a branch of the world tree, as a cedar seedling, but as a mustard seed: the smallest of seeds, the seed of a vegetable. Lydia's house—the house of a woman who sells purple fabrics and who has no proper name and a despised profession—is the center of the new life that empowers people to bring about justice. This justice is initiated when a meal is shared in the living quarters of a woman who sells purple fabrics. Here, one of the last had already become one of the first.[1]

Note

1. For the socio-historical material on which this essay is based, see Strabo, 13.630 (13.4.14); Pliny the Elder, *Naturalis historia* 9.125ff.; H. Blümner, *Technologie und Terminologie der Gewerbe und Künste bei Griechen und Römern* (Leipzig, 1912; Hildesheim, 1969), 1:225–48; N. Kampen, *Image and Status: Roman Working Women in Ostia* (Berlin, 1981), 133; Plutarch, *Pericles* 1; Martial, 9.62; *Diocletian's Maximal Tariff* 24.1ff.

6

The Woman Who Loved Much and the Pharisee Simon (Luke 7:36–50)

The purpose of the following reflections is an exegesis of the above text that deals in a nuanced way with Christian anti-Judaism and Christian sexism. I do not think an exegesis of this text that is fair to both women and Jews is easily accomplished. After all, the anti-Jewish and sexist traditions of Christianity in theology and Christian practice are rooted quite deeply. A non-sexist and a non–anti-Jewish exegesis remains a distant goal, and the following exegesis is only a small start on this long journey.

When it comes to women, the Christian tradition of dealing with prostitutes is connected with this text. According to this tradition, the proper path for these prostitutes is first to repent of their prostitution, whereby prostitution is primarily viewed as a moral—and not as a social—problem. This idea of the prostitute's repentance has pervasively influenced the Christian view of women—a fact that will be seen when examining the Christian scholarly interpretation of this text.

The disqualifying view of Judaism as an inferior religion finds expression in the contrast between the merciful Jesus and the law-abiding, hence merciless and self-righteous, Pharisee. Here, too, I shall critically examine the exegetical tradition. In addition, the text offers the particular nuance that Jesus tells the parable of two debtors. The contention that Judaism describes God as a pedant in financial matters, who calculates the earnings of people down to the last penny, is an anti-Judaic Christian commonplace. It is also quite interesting to observe how Christian exegetes deal with the fact that *Jesus* compares God to a creditor and has no problems relating an amount of money to an amount of love. A liberal English Jew, C. G. Montefiore, has described quite precisely the problem in his commentary (1927): "If [this passage] occurred in the Talmud, how theologians like J. Weiss would have been down on it. Is gratitude to be reckoned by the mere size of the service? How Jewish! So much service, so much gratitude. How Rabbinical!"[1]

I shall not discuss here the relationship between Luke 7:36–50 and Mark 14:3–9 par. Although Luke 7:36–50 is related to the narratives of the anointing in Bethany in a tradition-historical sense, it is, in relation to these narratives, an independent story. The story's profile in the context of the Gospel of Luke will be the focus of this examination, not possible hypotheses on the story's prior literary history. Also, I will disregard the later ecclesiological identification of Mary Magdalene with the woman in Luke 7:36–50, since Luke 7:36–50 does not intend such an identification. Mary Magdalene is introduced for the first time in Luke 8:2.

The Pharisee Simon

In this story, the Pharisee Simon is described as a host interested in Jesus (v. 36, invitation; v. 40, address, *didaskale*). In verses 44–46, the contrasting of his behavior to that of the woman does not intend to imply that the guest can, as a matter of course, expect foot-washing, a kiss, and an anointing of the head with oil and that, for this reason, Simon is treating Jesus in an improper, loveless, or provocative way. Nevertheless, the narrative uses the Pharisee as a figure of contrast.

On the one hand, his behavior stands in contrast to the behavior of Jesus: In verse 39, Jesus allows himself to be touched; the Pharisee presupposes that one does not allow oneself to be touched by a woman sinner. Of course, the hearer of the story knows that Jesus does not act out of ignorance, as the Pharisee, naively yet wrongly, assumes. In addition, Jesus' conversation with the Pharisee in verses 40–47, which constitutes the main part of the story, presents Jesus as instructing the Pharisee about his wrong perception of the woman and God's forgiveness. Although Jesus' discourse is wooing the Pharisee, the Pharisee remains a straw figure, a dummy, on whom something is to be demonstrated—namely, the contrast between Jesus' behavior and that of the Pharisee. The Pharisee does not emerge, in spite of his proper name, Simon, as an individual but as a representative of Pharisees *and* as a representative of wrong (un-Jesuslike) behavior.

On the other hand, the Pharisee is also a contrast-figure to the woman sinner. Her love and exuberance stand in contrast with the Pharisee's aloofness. Also the inserted parable of the debtors interprets the situation of the Pharisee as in contrast to the woman's situation.

Paradoxically, the Pharisee is poorer than the woman: He owes less, so God has to forgive him less; he loves less (v. 47b). Although he has less sin, he is poorer—in terms of received forgiveness and love.

Many of the parables employ such measures of contrast. The basic question is, then, whether such parables relate the contrast of *right and wrong* to certain *groups of people*.[2] If the parable of the feast in Luke 14:15–24 par. identifies the guests who had been invited first as the Jewish people or as a certain group of the Jews (such as the Pharisees), then the parable is anti-Judaistic in its root. Then, the church as a religious institution would view itself to be the group acting correctly in God's eyes or as the one loved by God, and it would set itself in contrast to those who act incorrectly. The interpretation of such contrasting measures in parables would completely differ, however, if the application of these contrasts were to remain open and the judgment of right or wrong were intended in an eschatological sense: God's judgment will reveal who the haughty first-invited guests were and who the true children of God. In that case, the parable intends to prompt people not to act incorrectly.

Since the parable of Luke 7:41–42 is embedded in a narrative, the parable loses the possible eschatological open-endedness. The Pharisee is the one acting wrongly, the one loving little. Nothing remains open here, as also is the case mainly in Luke 18:9–14 (which differs from the treatment in Luke 14:15–24), although Luke 7:36–50 deals less harshly with the Pharisees than Luke 18:9–14, where Pharisees are accused of despising all people except themselves. While viewing Luke 18:9–14 as a caricature of Pharisaism,[3] I can here at least reflect on whether Simon is depicted as a caricature or whether he is depicted in such a way that Pharisees living in his day could have recognized themselves in him. I cannot imagine the latter: Then, Pharisees would have had to accept that loving behavior toward *Jesus* alone was the correct way in God's eyes. Hence, the story might be a caricature, perhaps not as harsh as that in Luke 18:9–14, but still a caricature that uses the Pharisees as a negative foil for Jesus and the correct behavior toward Jesus. Unfortunately, I cannot but conclude, therefore, that we find here an incipient anti-Judaism, no matter how reticent the portrait of the Pharisee as someone interested and polite.

Nevertheless, the anti-Judaism in Luke 7:36–50 is by far not as comprehensive and complete as the anti-Judaism of the text's history of interpretation, and I refer here also to twentieth-century Christian scholarly interpretation. The anti-Judaism of exegetical history comes to the conclusion that Pharisaism "cannot forgive,"[4] and hence uses a contrast: On the one hand, Jesus proclaims God's unconditional mercy and forgiveness; on the other, Pharisaism (or Judaism) does not know anything, or not enough, of God's forgiveness. Quite frequently, exegetical history tries not to appear downright anti-Pharisaic in a caricaturist sense. In addition, some authors are aware that also Jewish texts speak of the comprehensive forgiveness of God. Yet it is all the more embarrassing, since less convincing, to see the contrast follow: Jesus' message of mercy versus Pharisaic or Jewish piety.

I shall illustrate this kind of anti-Judaism by means of a few exegetical examples. I should not like to disqualify the respective authors by doing so. Although one cannot excuse that we Christians have this exegetical tradition, one will have to admit that none of us can simply leave behind this kind of Christian thought and wash our hands in innocence. We have a long way to go—certainly, in little steps and many mistaken ideas. I include myself here. After all, I, too, come from this tradition, and it has taken me a long time to realize the connection between Christian theology—including my own—and Auschwitz. I think it utterly important for today's Christian-theological (and also for the feminist-theological) discussion that we continue to work on this inexcusable tradition of our theology. I think it similarly important also for female feminist theologians arguing in an anti-Judaistic fashion—as well as for the male theologians who will be cited in the following—to observe how they deal with this kind of anti-Judaism *after* they become, or have been made, aware of it. It should be clear, though, that subconscious anti-Judaism is not to be excused here either.

No one who has heard of Walter Grundmann's national-socialist activities will be surprised to see him exegete this text in an anti-Judaistic fashion.[5] The firm rootage of Christian anti-Judaism in all of Christian theology, however, is illuminated by the fact that a national-socialist theologian (or a formerly national-socialist theologian) with his anti-Judaistic interpretation formulates the *consensus* of scholarly exegetical tradition up to the present time. Grundmann's commentaries are found in the libraries of any of today's seminaries that train male and female theologians and are usually consulted by students without their being aware of the problem. The awareness of the problem cannot come about as long as those women and men receive no historical information about Grundmann and as long as their instructors hold the same ideas as Grundmann. With Grundmann, they reach their pinnacle in the sentence: "It is the relation to the sinner and the proclamation of unconditional forgiveness where the Pharisees part company with Jesus."[6] Correspondingly, Grundmann makes a connection between the parable of the debtors in Luke 7:41–42 and rabbinic theology ("as, in general, the merchant's characteristics are of great importance for the rabbinic picture of God"), but still sees in this parable Jesus breaking away from this tradition. The creditor remits both debtors of their debts. Grundmann comments: "This surprising turn of events points to Jesus' message: God does not want to be the harsh creditor who extorts debt payments, but the forgiving father who forgives debt. At this point, the father image of Jesus emerges" (p. 171). Here, the exegete *no longer* points to the connection between the parable of the debtors and rabbinic tradition, which views God as the generous creditor also.[7] Thus, the entire anti-Judaism hides already behind the word "surprising": The God of Jesus forgives debt, while the Jewish God lists debt. The Pharisee Simon issues his own verdict (7:43) "without his knowing that he has issued his own verdict" (pp. 171–72). The picture of Christian anti-Judaism in this interpretation has to be completed by the observation that it tries to stay clear of vulgar anti-Pharisaism as if aware of the problems involved in that. Grundmann comments on the beginning of the story (7:36): "Here, a relationship between Jesus and the Pharisees is made visible that is not hostile from the very start. Jesus accepts the invitation and, hence, does not see himself *on his part* in an unbridgeable contrast to the Pharisees" (p. 170). Thus, the anti-Judaistic principle—the God of Jesus forgives unconditionally, the God of the Pharisees does not but calculates like a merchant—is established by remaining silent on one part of Jewish tradition. In addition, this principle contains the subtle argument that the contrast between Judaism and Christianity is not Jesus' fault (and that means also: not the Christians' fault) but the fault of the Jews, who are responsible for the contrast and pronounce their own verdict.

One will have to ask the question now whether Grundmann is correct with this interpretation—that is, if his anti-Judaism simply reflects in an exegetically correct way the anti-Judaism of this *text*. I see an important difference between the anti-Judaism of Grundmann and the one in Luke 7:36–50. In Luke 7:36–50, Jesus does not proclaim a new doctrine of God and God's unconditional forgiveness; rather, he applies the idea of a forgiving God, which is *common* to both Jesus and the Pharisee, to a concrete situation, namely to a situation where the Pharisee Simon (the way the text portrays him) would not apply this idea of the forgiving God: Jesus does not avoid the touch by the woman sinner, although he agrees with the Pharisee that she is a sinner or a debtor. Furthermore, Jesus views the boundless love of her life as a prostitute *and* her turning to him as an expression of having experienced God's forgiveness (for the basis of this thesis, see below). Hence, the text is not about the difference between the Pharisee's concept of God and that of Jesus, but about the difference between the way they relate to prostitutes. The Jesus of this story does not fear becoming unclean and does not expect prostitutes to give up their lives as prostitutes as the consequence of God's forgiveness. But that is precisely the assumption of Christian theological exegesis, unstated in Grundmann but often stated openly elsewhere: Give up that life! On the question of how a Christian is to treat prostitutes, the behavior of the Pharisee Simon might be more representative for the later Christian ecclesiological practice than the behavior of Jesus. Although the ideas on purification were no longer relevant to Christianity in the way they were to Jewish tradition, one finds among Christians regulations concerning prostitutes that are even more rigid than those of cultic purification (the way this text presupposes it); in cultic purification the uncleanness can at least be washed off (Leviticus 15). Although the Pharisee of this narrative is a straw figure because he is used as a figure of contrast (see above), he is not a straw figure representing a wrong Pharisaic *theology* (God concept); rather, he represents *a certain behavior toward prostitutes*. The anti-Judaism of Grundmann's interpretation is intertwined with sexism since Grundmann does not say that God can forgive prostitutes unconditionally. He much rather speaks *in general* of the "relation to the sinner and the proclamation of unconditional forgiveness" (p. 173).

The interpretation by Grundmann is no more anti-Judaistic than any other Christian interpretation I found. I shall cite a few examples: Heinz Schürmann talks of the "unheard-of new [thing] that now has come into the world." In the parable, Jesus supposedly "assumes, at first, the viewpoint of Pharisaism, which knew both the 'just' and the 'sinner'..., as well as 'great' and 'small' sinners without realizing that even the 'just' still had to pray: 'God have mercy on me, a sinner.'" He assumes that "the parable argues here from the basis of that insufficient position in order to direct one's gaze to the 'advantages' for the repentant sinner, which Pharisaism—and the self-righteous heart of people of all times—continued to ignore."[8] It is an "insufficient" concept of God's forgiveness and self-righteousness—and thereby an exemplary case of all human self-righteousness—that forms the basis for the anti-Judaistic criticism of the interpretation. A basic difference in treating the problem does not exist between Grundmann and Schürmann. Still, Schürmann is a little more explicit in his treatment of the woman sinner: She is the *converted* sinner; details of her past had been omitted in the text "so that the general aspect of the new [ecclesiological] situation remains open in it: the reception of [converted] sinners into the community of Jesus and—later on and to this day—into the church" (p. 432). No attempt is made to critically analyze one's own perspective: Such is the perspective of Christians who look down on, and from a distance at, Jews. The fact that the centuries-old political superiority and power over Jews is at play here becomes plain in the utter absence of any attempt to deal with Jewish traditions the way Jews see them. The prostitute, too, is the mere object of a perspective that controls the power of definition and of social superiority, which imposes repentance on women in misery. By generalizing and directing the theological interpretation to all sinners, one distracts from the concrete fate of the respective women.

The first part of Schürmann's commentary on Luke was written at a time when in both parts of Germany the discussion on Christian anti-Judaism at theological faculties and schools was completely ignored. The book appeared in 1969. Yet even in more recent works, the picture does not show much change. As an example, I shall choose Eduard Schweizer's interpretation (1982).[9] The Pharisee Simon appears here as a correct, careful, and distant onlooker, whom Jesus woos with the parable. In the description of the Pharisee, one finds here a choice of words that is more careful than in older commentaries. In terms of content, however, I see no difference to exegetical tradition. Schweizer says: "However, both [the woman and the Pharisee] are guilty, and since the Pharisee cannot, for theological reasons, admit to that, as his carefully formulated answer indicates (18:11), he becomes (18:14) the truly guilty one and is even unable to 'show less love' (vv. 44, 46)." That means: The Pharisee becomes the truly guilty one since he has a theology for which the law is the way of salvation so that he does not feel dependent on God's mercy. Hence, we find also here the unbroken exegetical tradition that considers law and love as opposing alternatives. The old Christian accusation that Pharisees are self-righteous emerges also, though in a verbally softer form ("self-sufficiency, . . . which does not seem to need anything").

Eduard Schweizer describes the prostitute with obvious patriarchal sympathy, though "she no longer is a respectable lady." He says: Her behavior is "fearful, clumsy, and a little awkward." The scene also appears "to be erotically colored and may show an element of hysteria." The "woman may be unable to intellectually express her more or less clear self-awareness, yet she finds her way to Jesus by her actions." She becomes the model of repentance of those "who cast themselves away in self-pity and resigned willfulness," who "only find meaning in the consumption of alcohol and drugs, in chronic illness, or in prostitution." Since she has repented, it is assumed here that she no longer will live as a prostitute: "At all times, salvation seeks to take a visible form."

The Woman Sinner

The woman sinner of Luke 7:36–50 becomes, according to Christa Mulack,[10] the "female representative of Sephardic rights; in her is expressed what commonly is assumed to be *typically female*. All four evangelists contrast her with something that they, too, must have perceived to be *typically male*" (p. 303). Mulack does not consider the fact that the woman in Luke 7:36ff. is a prostitute; she considers only her "sinfulness," which is generalized in words chosen from Walter Nigg: "Men enjoy sinning with the woman, though afterwards they scorn the abused woman as a sinner and do not see that they themselves have become guilty also." Very many women who are—or should be—at pains to keep distance between themselves and prostitutes can supposedly identify with this description of the "woman sinner." Mulack heavily stresses the contrast between the woman's behavior and male ideas: "This woman fits neither in patriarchal-religious nor in patriarchal-scientific world views" (p. 303); "she...did not at all seem to fit into the male thought pattern" (p. 304). The male structures are supposed to be represented by the disciples (as in Mark 14:3–8) and by Pharisees (as in Luke 7:36–50). Christa Mulack unites the four versions of the anointment story in a kind of Gospel harmony, from which she then comments regarding the version of Luke 7:36ff. (though the latter is quite autonomous). The Pharisee supposedly represents the "male" mind (p. 305) and produces an "atmosphere" turned "rigid by the law and [its] coldness" (p. 304).

The main structures of the dominating exegetical tradition are partially maintained here. Also maintained is its anti-Judaism (which is not neutralized even by the fact that the male disciples receive the same reproaches as the Pharisees) as well as the generalization that distracts from the concrete story and the actual social experiences. This generalization differs when applied to the *women* abused by men (instead of to all "sinners") as does the contrasting of good and evil as female and male. The narrative is read as the story of a woman who has been abused by men and who is grateful and loves boundlessly after she has experienced Jesus' liberation. Her kisses and tears, her open, soft hair ("What a repulsive sexual symbol!" [p. 304]) wash Jesus clean and enable him to "perform this symbolic act [feet washing] on his disciples." I shall not criticize this interpretation because it ignores historical questions but because of what it contains. Prevalent exegesis appropriates Luke 7:36ff. to the disadvantage of prostitutes and Jews (or Pharisees) and offers the middle-class individual the pleasant assurance that God loves sinners, no matter what they did. This feminist interpretation appropriates the text to the disadvantage of prostitutes and Pharisees—and then also of men at large, in which procedure the anti-Judaistic accusations are much in foreground ("law"; "rigid atmosphere"; and, in general, the consistent antithesis of love and law). The interpretation wants to give women the feeling that they "are people created for love" (p. 303, citing Nigg). The woman "does not love by words but by her entire being" (p. 304). With this interpretation, the role of women so desired by men is perfect. What patriarchal man would not enjoy having this unlimited, orgiastic, emotional love at his feet and empowering him? There is a difference—and I do not ignore it—between whether it is Christian middle-class individuals who draw strength from this tradition or women whose femininity is celebrated here. I only doubt whether this kind of encouragement of women (to the disadvantage of Jews and other men) produces, in reality, something else but simply a new attire for the role of women that patriarchal society so desires. The close resemblance of Eduard Schweizer's portrayal of the prostitute and Christa Mulack's only supports this assumption.

In Mulack's case, the actual history of women in violent society and the actual story of prostitutes, of which this narrative tells, are ignored in the same way as the reality of Jewish women and men. The actions attributed to the woman are: loving, warming, cleansing, kissing, wasting—in a word "what women do" (p. 306). The men with their psychic deformation (money hunger, profit-oriented thinking, moral concepts) are called on to be like Jesus: to take a stand for female and against male attributes and to become empowered by the love of women.

I could not find a feminist-theological interpretation that takes seriously the fact that the woman in the text is a prostitute.

The Prostitute

Some exegetes have denied that the woman sinner (*hamartōlos*) in Luke 7:36–50 was a prostitute.[11] Yet, in my view, the text wants to say that she is a prostitute. My arguments are the following:

1. *Verse 37:* A "woman sinner *in the city*"[12]—this formulation makes sense only when the city (*polis*) is considered as the social environment in which the woman is defined as a sinner. The opposing interpretation views the phrase "in the city" as a marginal note that simply tells that the woman comes from the city where Jesus is at the time. Yet such a note would be superfluous and would have no meaning in the context.

2. *Verse 47:* One finds here the parallel of her "many

sins" with her great love ("for she has loved much"). Although the comment "for she has loved much" has often been interpreted as a summary of her love (vv. 37ff.) for Jesus, the reference to her "many sins," the emphasis on her many individual deeds, is intended to recall *also* the many love deeds the woman performed in her life as a prostitute. Thus, in my view, the central issue of the text is the interpretation of the manifold love of a prostitute as a life under God's forgiveness.

3. *Verses 37, 39:* One might say that both the word *hamartōlos*, assigned to the woman, and the taboo of touch could theoretically also refer to other forms of sinfulness. However, the fact that *a woman* is portrayed as *hamartōlos* produces the association with a specifically female kind of sinfulness—especially since we know the patriarchal conditions underpinning the texts of the New Testament.

4. *Matt. 21:31–32:* This text makes clear that prostitutes played a particular role in the Baptist's movement and in the Jesus movement. Even if one were not, for example out of feminist interest, to consider the woman in Luke 7:36–50 as a prostitute (since that would be typically "male thinking"), the basic problem remains that a particular connection existed between Jesus and prostitutes. For that reason, the decision whether the woman in Luke 7:36–50 is to be considered a prostitute is not appropriate as a decision of principle. It does not solve the "problem." Instead, one should ask whether a properly understood feminist interest would not *first* need to address prostitutes, thus repeating Jesus' own behavior.

The social-historical question of the *living conditions of prostitutes* at the time the text was written is the unavoidable basis for the text's interpretation. Women get into the work of prostitution usually for economic reasons. Widows and single women prostituted themselves (or their daughters) since that is the only way of achieving a remuneration of women's work that prevents starvation (in place of many proofs, see Lucian, *Hetärengespräche* 6). There is also such a thing as the downward "career":

First, women try to survive by working in textile industry; then, if they no longer can earn anything there, they work as prostitutes (Terence, *Andria* 70ff.). Next, one finds prostitutes who already as children were trained to prostitute themselves: as foundlings or slaves. Due to the economic hardship of many people in the Roman Empire, parents even sold their children into prostitution. One could extend this list of misery. In the large cities of the Roman Empire, prostitution reached enormous dimensions. For the area of Palestine, Josephus testifies of brothels in Sebaste and Caesarea (*Ant.* 19.357), yet probably with the idea that only the non-Jewish population had any dealings with these brothels. However, one is probably more correct to assume, as does Iwan Bloch, that organized prostitution was a Roman institution among the Jews of Jesus' time.[13]

One may correctly suspect, then, that Jewish *women* became the victims of prostitution, rather than Jewish men who went to prostitutes (a fact even Philo denies, Philo, *De Josepho* 43). A relevant rabbinic narrative exists that describes well the situation of prostitutes and clarifies also that Jesus' behavior—just as that of John the Baptist—is not "shocking" in the context of Judaism. Since this story is copied from the Jerusalem Talmud (*Ta'anit* 1.64.41) in Billerbeck (2:162), it is actually inexcusable that, despite this easily accessible information, Christian theologians should describe Jesus' behavior as unusual for Judaism. A mule driver is asked what good deeds he had done. He says: "Once, I leased my mule to a woman who began to cry on the way. I said to her: What is wrong with you? She replies: My husband has been arrested, and I want to see what I have to do to bail him out [she intends to engage in prostitution to use the money for bail]. I sold my mule, then, and I gave the money to her. I told her: This is yours, bail your husband out and do not sin."

The situation of prostitutes is understood here from the social perspective, not from the moral. Although prostitutes violate the will of God, hence are sinners, God forgives them and is pleased with those who prevent their hardship, such as the mule driver.

Also, Luke 7:36–50 tells of *God's mercy bestowed on the prostitute*—and *not of the repentance of the prostitute* as a condition or as a consequence of forgiveness. Exegetical history has discussed in great detail the question whether repentance is the condition or the consequence of forgiveness, since the text seems contradictory on this point. In our context, it may suffice to say that the text is, indeed, contradictory on this question because it takes no interest in the problem. In verse 47 (*hoti*), love is the *reason* (the actual reason) of forgiveness, which is more obvious linguistically than the proposal that the verse speaks of the *basis of awareness* (it is love that indicates that forgiveness was granted). In contrast, verses 41–42 and the end of verse 47 presuppose the reverse order, or causality: Love follows forgiveness.

It is important, however, to understand the action of the woman in verses 37b–38, which is later interpreted by Jesus in verses 44–50. What seems fundamental to me is that here repentance is not portrayed in the sense of turning away from prostitution. One might be able to assume that the brothers and sisters in the Jesus movement will have, like the mule driver, enabled the woman to live a life without prostitution out of their sense of economic solidarity; yet it certainly was not Jesus' or the Jesus movement's idea to demand that a person driven to sin out of hardship should convert in both the moral and the religious sense. Conversion—a turning away from sinning—is a matter of both practicality and economy, which certainly was not possible for this woman. The text, however, leaves all these questions open and does not tell of the prostitute's repentance but of a prostitute's love for Jesus.

The woman's action is described at great length and in great detail and dominates the narrative's flow. The rest is commentary on the action.

In verse 37b, the woman turns to Jesus because she

hopes to receive help from him (cf. Mark 5:27). Her situation is described as one of *distress,* as is expressed by her crying in verse 38. Her tears are not tears of repentance or gratitude (as the interpreters assume), but an expression of her distress before God and people (cf. the tears of the woman meeting the mule driver; see above). She is ostracized by uncleanliness both in the cultic and the social sense (cf. the taboo of touch). She can no longer put her distress into words. Although she does not say a word, she is (next to God, who forgives) the only one acting in the story. By this action, *she herself* opens up her distress.

Her behavior toward Jesus is just as dramatic as the way she gives expression to her distress. On the one hand, she takes her place by his feet like a slave (v. 38; cf. Seneca, *De beneficiis* 3.27.1). On the other hand, she bestows honors on Jesus like a hostess who wants to show the guest the utmost of respect: She honors him by washing and drying his feet (v. 38), by *proskynēsis,* by kissing his feet. Thus she honors him the way a hostess honors her guest and at the same time expresses her distress and her lowliness in an oddly extraneous way. Her tears are the water, her hair is the towel, her *proskynēsis* is the kisses on the feet. As we have seen, various commentaries point out the erotic side of her action—and justly so. Yet one will have to add: Jesus accepts the erotic touch of *a prostitute.* Anointing the feet after washing them is probably another step to increase the honor offered to the guest, who more commonly was anointed on the head (see v. 46); and she even takes especially costly oil, more costly than is usually custom (see the terminological difference between *elaion* and *myron,* v. 46; cf. v. 37). Jesus' response to her is nothing but affirming. He defends her, explains her behavior, and pronounces God's forgiveness over her, which presupposes that this forgiveness does not take place from a certain point on but that her entire life is accompanied by God's forgiveness. As a much-loving woman—both in relation to Jesus and in her life as a prostitute—she has received much forgiveness. She loves prodigiously, she suffers desperately, she is guilty before God, and she is God's beloved child. And it is this that Jesus tells those standing by and, in the end, also the woman directly. In no way does this story neatly divide the love of Jesus and the love of a prostitute, life under God's mercy now and sinful life then. These divisions appear only when looking (or when men look) at prostitutes from the point of view of a correctional institution,[14] from outside or from above. In this story, Jesus precisely does not make these particular distinctions.

The woman sinner who loved much is not the model of the converted sinner and not the *model* of the sinful woman. She is the *last* among the women who becomes the first, to use the imagery of the Jesus tradition. The destiny of the prostitute is that of the "last" in the sense of Jesus' words in Matt. 20:16 par. The connection between prostitution and the social role of "regular" women is often repressed even by women. How often are women expected to flirt, both in private or at the work place—how often are unpleasant situations created for women because they are eyed as "loose girls"! Prostitution is the extreme case of work done out of love, which is what is expected of women, even to this day. A position of power defines the availability of women, which in the social role of the prostitute appears only clearer than in the role of "regular" women, who are viewed as accessible in some other way.

In summary: The text of Luke 7:36–50 treats the situation of the woman sinner in a more differentiated and just manner than that of the Pharisee Simon. Still, both the woman and the Pharisee are treated with contempt in exegetical history. The road to justice to Jews and women is still a long one for Christians.

Notes

1. C. G. Montefiore, *The Synoptic Gospels*, 2d ed. (London: Macmillan & Co., 1927), 2:431.
2. See L. Schottroff, "Das Gleichnis vom grossen Gastmahl in der Logienquelle," *EvT* 47 (1987): 192–211.
3. L. Schottroff, "Die Erzählung vom Pharisäer und Zöllner als Beispiel für die theologische Kunst des Überredens," in *Neues Testament und christliche Existenz: Festschrift für Herbert Braun* (Tübingen, 1973), 439–61.
4. G. Eichholz, *Gleichnisse der Evangelien* (Neukirchen, 1971), 64 (quote by Schlatter). To Eichholz, Pharisaism is the prototype of middle-class and of ecclesial society. Yet there is, in my view, a contradiction in Eichholz when he says: "Our common ideas of Pharisaism need a correction" (p. 59). A. Schlatter says: "The separation between the Pharisee and Jesus results from the fact that for the former there was no way to the guilty" (*Das Evangelium des Lukas* [Stuttgart, 1931], 258; see also 357).
5. See L. Siegele-Wenschkewitz, "Mitverantwortung und Schuld der Christen am Holocaust," *EvT* 42 (1982): 171–80.
6. W. Grundmann, *Das Evangelium nach Lukas*, 5th ed. (Berlin, 1969), 173.
7. See H. Strack and P. Billerbeck, *Das Evangelium nach Matthäus: Kommentar zum Neuen Testament*, 1:421.
8. H. Schürmann, *Das Lukasevangelium*, HTKNT 3 (1969), 1:434.
9. E. Schweizer, *Das Evangelium nach Lukas*, NTD 3 (Göttingen, 1982), on that passage.
10. C. Mulack, *Die Weiblichkeit Gottes*, 2d ed. (Stuttgart, 1983).
11. For example, Schlatter, *Lukas*, who calls her the "woman of a sinner."

12. Reading the text as *gynē en tē polei hētis ēn hamartōlos* is, text-historically speaking, a later rendering and already an attempt to distinguish between information about the city and information about the woman's sinfulness and to view her existence as a sinner in a more general sense.

13. I. Bloch, *Die Prostitution* (Berlin, 1912), 1:602–4.

14. John Chrysostom says on Matt. 21:31–32: "As long as they remain prostitutes, they may not enter; only when they obey, believe, cleanse themselves, and repent" (*Homily on Matthew* 67).

7

The Virgin Birth
(Luke 1:26–33, 38)

The announcement of Jesus' birth according to the annunciation narratives of the New Testament (Luke 1:26–38; Matt. 1:18–25) is fraught with obstacles to understanding.[1] The first obstacle is the—warranted—question, raised in the Enlightenment, whether Christians have to consider as true something that cannot be true according to their knowledge of biology. One should not evade this warranted question, in my view. Men and women who proclaim the gospel need not impose on anyone a *sacrificium intellectus*. They can clarify also in their sermons that one does not *have to* believe such a miracle if one is unable to do so. Only after this clarification, the obstacle for understanding this New Testament tradition is removed, and one can ask what the virgin birth meant then and what it can mean to believers now.

The second obstacle is the history of the Marian dogma and the veneration of Mary,[2] which even in Protestantism today has not remained without consequences. On the one hand, Mariology is present primarily in the iconographic tradition (see, for example, the well-known annunciation of the Isenheim Altar); on the other hand, the Protestant critique of Catholic Mariology may still play an important role, mainly through the fact that Luke 1:26–38 is primarily read as a christological text and only secondarily as a Mariological one. In the contemporary women's movement, the critique of Mariology addresses particularly the juxtaposition of Eve, the mother of sinful humanity, and Mary, the mother of the savior. This juxtaposition corresponds to that of sinful (wife or) woman and sinless virgin, or in general, to that of sinful sexuality and sinless virginity. As long as the word "virgin" (Luke 1:27) is associated with the degradation of (female) sexuality, the understanding of the text is impaired. Neither Luke 1:26–38 nor Matt. 1:18–25 sees a contrast between the virgin Mary and the wife of Joseph, the mother of Joseph's children, who Mary is, according to all Gospels (see Luke 8:19–21 par.; Matt. 13:55–57 par.).[3] The New Testament does not see Mary's virginity as a kind of purity that stands in contrast with impure sexuality. As far as I can tell, resistance to church tradition is so strong at this point that it must first be shown that the text is neither antiwomen nor downgrading of sexuality, following which one can then ask in what sense sexuality is understood in the text and how believers today can take this tradition up productively.

Now, I should like to explain the text historically by exegeting it verse by verse. From the historical explanation, then, I shall draw conclusions for a contemporary understanding of the virgin birth.

Verse 26: Earlier, the angel Gabriel had announced to Zechariah the miraculous birth of a son (see Luke 1:11, 19). Zechariah and his wife, Elizabeth, are an old, childless couple (Luke 1:7). The miracle of the birth of their child, John (the Baptist), is the repetition of the miraculous birth of Isaac to the infertile Sarah (Gen. 16:1; 17:17, 19; etc.) and of the miraculous birth of Samuel to the infertile Hannah (1 Sam. 1:1ff.). The miraculous opening of the infertile woman's womb by God's doing is, according to the Old Testament and Jewish tradition, a miracle of God where the lowly are elevated (see the Song of Hannah in 1 Sam. 2:1–10).

On the one hand, the miraculous births of John the Baptist and of Jesus are narrated as mutually connected, parallel miracles of God. The sixth month, when Gabriel visits Mary (v. 26), is the sixth month of pregnancy for Elizabeth (see 1:24, 36). Both are miraculous deeds of God (v. 37). On the other hand, the birth of Jesus is the birth of the Messiah, while the birth of John the Baptist is the birth of the forerunner (see, e.g., the jumping of the unborn child John the Baptist in the pregnant womb of his mother when she meets the pregnant Mary [Luke 1:41, 44]). The miracle of Jesus' birth is even greater than that of John's birth, a miracle in which the birth by an infertile woman is escalated to the birth by a virgin.

Verse 27: Mary is engaged to Joseph. This "engagement" is the legally binding first act of marriage. The young woman remains still in her parents' house. After about one year, the man takes the woman to his house. Only during this second act of marriage, sexual relations begin. Yet already in the first act of marriage, the young woman is legally a wife and all that that entails, as in case, for example, of adultery, divorce, or death of the partner.[4]

Joseph is David's descendant. Because of Joseph, who is not the natural father, Jesus too is David's descendant (see Luke 1:32). In the social and legal sense, Joseph is the father of the child (see also Luke 3:23–28 with Jesus' genealogy according to Luke) and Jesus, thus, David's son. Neither Matthew nor Luke had a problem here with Jesus' being a son of David.

Mary's virginity at this point of marriage, hence, is "normal." Since her virginity is mentioned twice in verse 27, one sees that it is already clear to both narrator and listener that the angel is not announcing the birth of a child from the commenced marriage but the *birth of a child without bodily father, a child not procreated.* Mary has known this very fact too, according to the narrative (see v. 37). The pregnancy of the infertile Elizabeth is topped by the miracle occurring to Mary. Hence, for an understanding of this narrative, much depends on how one interprets virginity. The text does not say in the least that sexual intercourse causes one to be unclean or that virginity means purity. The latter interpretation has emerged only under Hellenistic influence beginning with the second century. The text says: It is a miracle when a woman becomes pregnant *without the participation of a man.* Only the ensuing dogmatic interest in Jesus' and, hence, Mary's sinlessness has interpreted Mary's virginity in a sense of animosity toward sexuality and women. This reinterpretation has led to attempts in which one tries to find Mary's perpetual virginity in Luke 1:24 (as in Matt. 1:25).[5]

The text itself shows that the virginity of Mary in Luke 1:26–28 is not meant to be antiwomen since the text stresses the miracle of the fatherless birth. The discussion concerning the origin of the idea of virgin birth has pursued primarily the question of which ideas of *divine procreation* existed in the environment of the New Testament. One generally finds that the virgin birth according to Luke and Matthew is narrated as divine procreation, as in the cases of Alexander the Great or Plato, where a god and a human woman are the parents. One also finds that it is absolutely foreign to the Old Testament and to Judaism to view God as a procreating man. Nevertheless, in spite of it all, one still seems to expect a procreation carried out by God or the Spirit.[6] The Greek word *gennaō* signifies both to father and to give birth. It is inappropriate to the texts to translate this word in Luke 1:35 and Matt. 1:20 as "fathering," as the Zürcher Bible has done, among others; instead, one should translate it as "creating." One will have to discuss the Spirit's role of creation when dealing with verse 35. Yet already at this point, it should be clear that the meaning of the text is that Mary becomes pregnant without the act of procreation. Neither a human man nor any other conceivably manlike divine creature participated here in a procreating fashion.

Verse 28: "Greetings" is an everyday Greek salutation. Mary is *kecharitōmenē,* one who has been favored since she has "found favor with God" (v. 30), and the Lord is with her (v. 28). Mary's finding favor with God is the elevation of a lowly person (see Luke 1:48), the election of a woman who is to become God's entryway into the world, God's entryway to becoming human.

Verses 30–33: Both pregnancy and birth are viewed here, as also in the continuation of Luke's birth narrative, as any "normal" pregnancy and birth. Thereby, it becomes clear again that Jesus' birth is not associated with the negative connotation of sexuality and of women. The New Testament stories do not take away any of the pregnancy's and birth's bodiliness. Mary is not an ethereal being but a woman who is connected to another human being with her body. This quite normal young woman is to be the place where God becomes human; she is to be the home for the life-creating Spirit (v. 35). Mary is a woman and, as such, her people show her little respect both socially and culturally. She is a Jewish woman and part of an oppressed and suffering people (see Luke 4:18). And she is among the poor of her people, the country population of Galilee (see v. 26) who are hard pressed by the daily experience of economic hardship. The pregnancy with the Messiah and Son of God brings the most lowly and the most exalted in the world together. The Messiah is the Son of God, and his royal reign comprises heaven and earth. His reign will never end. This merciful king over heaven and earth, God's son, is born to a country woman from Galilee. The mystery of God's becoming human is not described in abstract terms—in concepts or circumscriptions—but as an event with all its everyday, small, and physical aspects.

The Virgin Birth (Luke 1:26–33, 38)

It is important for Western European theology, with its abstract world of ideas, to experience with the text the physical and small aspects of God's becoming human. During the weeks and months of the spring and summer of 1986, after the Chernobyl reactor accident, women's bodily connectedness with future generations through pregnancy, their connectedness through their children with the grass, with trees and the sand, was experienced like a painful wound of humanity. The tenderness and vulnerability of all humans become visible in pregnant women: Today just as then, awareness of this may be lost once in a while. Mary's pregnancy with the king of the world shows how God bonds with the people, namely, where they are most vulnerable and weak. Here, Matthew says "God with us" (Matt. 1:23) and expresses what Luke says, too. The Magnificat of Mary calls this event the elevation of the lowly. The pregnant Mary is the representative of all the powerless, of all the hungry, of all despised women, whose bodies God does not overlook (Luke 1:46–54).

Jesus' titles of honor (Luke 1:32ff.) refer to Old Testament texts (mainly Isa. 9:5–10; 2 Samuel 7; Dan. 7:14), indicating thereby that Jesus is the Davidic Messiah, promised by God in scripture, who henceforth and forever will rule over the people of God. Here, as in the other Synoptic Gospels, the future royal reign of God begins with Jesus. This Messiah, longingly expected by a suffering people, has come; the royal reign of God has come, as small still as a mustard seed (Luke 13:18–19 par.). With the Messiah's birth, death, and resurrection, God has acted on behalf of humans. They find God's closeness in the pregnant Mary, among the hungry, among the blind, and they lift up their heads "for your salvation is near" (Luke 21:28). According to the Gospels, as here in Luke's annunciation story, people believe in God's closeness. The academic "dogma" concerning the delay of the parousia has only impeded the understanding of God's nearness. God is not remote for Luke or for today's Christians—as long as they still hope for the royal reign of God, which began with the pregnancy of a poor woman.

On verse 34: See above on verses 26 and 27.

Verse 35: Neither the word *eperchesthai,* coming down, nor *episkiazein,* overshadow, has an implied sexual connotation.[7] For people associated with the Jewish religion and its language, the Spirit (*ruach*) is female anyway; the Greek noun *pneuma* is neuter and is not connected with ideas of a person or manhood either. With God's Spirit are connected ideas of wind, breath, the vibrating of a bird's wings; creation (not procreation) is associated with the Spirit's life-giving power. Old Testament references concerning a renewed enlivening, a renewed creation by the Spirit of God, are found in Ezek. 37:1-14; Job 32:8; 33:4; and Pss. 33:6; 104:30.[8] New Testament parallels on the subject are mainly in John 1:13 and John 3:1-8. The new creature that the Spirit creates is the Messiah Jesus in his greatness and his smallness. He is connected as a vulnerable human being with other human beings but also as a new creation of the Spirit: Believers, too, can become children of God through the Spirit (see, for example, the story of Pentecost in Acts 2:1ff.).

New Testament Christianity experienced the activity of the Spirit, the Spirit's enlivening, strengthening, and changing power among the believers. A close connection exists between the event of the virgin birth and the event where believers are endowed with spiritual gifts. As long as the birth story of Jesus is viewed as a story about majesty, it shuts the door to heaven. Only when the connection between the Spirit-created Messiah and the people who are visited by God's Spirit is experienced will the affirmation of Christ's unending rule have any truth. Nothing is as democratic as the Holy Spirit (see also 1 Cor. 12:3ff.) and the Spirit's life-giving power, of which the birth narrative tells.

On verses 36 and 37: See above on verses 26ff.

Verse 38: Mary's obedience to God's will means, according to the understanding of the Gospel of Luke, that she is the first of Jesus' disciples (see 8:21). One should not confuse this obedience with submission. Obedience to God's will does not destroy one's self-confidence but builds it up (see the Magnificat).

From reading Luke 1:26–38, I cannot see that Christology and Mariology are opposed to each other. Mary's pregnancy, her bearing the king of heaven and earth in her womb, puts God in the most vulnerable of places among people. It is God's intention that the salvation of the world begin in the womb of a poverty-ridden woman and not in executive boardrooms. God bestows high value on the pregnant woman and on the real world, endangered as it is. The false culture of men, which still views God in heaven as the reflection of male sexuality and world conquest, finds expression in such ideas as that of procreation by a god, which is not only foreign to Jewish and Christian tradition in its origins but is also rejected by it. A humanitarian community of men and women evolves whenever people start looking for God's rule and closeness in the vulnerable bodies of people.

In this sense, the virgin birth is a God-wrought miracle that strengthens today's people on their journey to God's royal reign. Both preacher and congregation share the hunger for experiencing the life-giving power of the Holy Spirit in a threatened world. Mary's experience, described in the text, corresponds to this hunger, responds to a longing, and awakens the imagination to seek and share with each other analogous experiences. It is important also for men practicing faith today to act like Mary, like a pregnant woman: to take care of life, to guard it, and to preserve the bodies of other people.

Notes

1. When I wrote this essay, the important book by J. Schaberg, *The Illegitimacy of Jesus: A Feminist Theological Interpretation of the Infancy Narratives* (New York: Harper & Row, 1987), had not yet appeared. Even though I am in accord with her basic tendency and many of her individual observations, I am not able to discern, as she does, an awareness of an illegitimate pregnancy of Mary's on the part of the infancy narratives' authors. It is for that reason that I maintain the interpretation of the texts presented now; I intend to discuss her book extensively elsewhere.

2. For an overview, see, for example, K. Onasch and W. Jannasch, "Marienverehrung," and J. Weerda, "Mariologie," in *RGG*, 3d ed., 4:763–66; 767–70.

3. See R. R. Ruether, *Mary, the Feminine Face of the Church* (Philadelphia: Westminster Press, 1977), 37ff.

4. Besides the commentaries on Luke 1:27 and Matt. 1:18, see especially H. L. Strack and P. Billerbeck, *Kommentar zum Neuen Testament aus Talmud und Midrasch* (Munich, 1924), 2:393–98.

5. See the references on exegetical history in R. E. Brown et al., eds., *Mary in the New Testament* (Philadelphia: Fortress Press, 1978), 107ff.; and U. Luz, *Das Evangelium nach Matthäus*, EKKNT 1/1 (1985), 108.

6. See, for example, M. Dibelius, "Jungfrauensohn und Krippenkind: Untersuchungen zur Geburtsgeschichte Jesu im Lukas-Evangelium" (1932) in Dibelius, *Botschaft und Geschichte* (1953), 1:1–78. He acknowledges the rejection of ideas of theogamy in Judaism (p. 33) and calls Mary's conception a "counterimage of human procreation" (p. 19), but still presupposes a Hellenistic influence and some kind of procreation

by God or the Spirit resulting from this influence (pp. 35ff.). See also Brown et al., eds., *Mary*, 102, with n. 275; in spite of the conclusion that the case cannot be considered a theogamy, there is talk about the procreation of God.

7. See, for example, Brown et al., eds., *Mary*, 102.

8. For further references, see, for example, A. Paul, *L'évangile de l'enfance selon saint Matthieu* (Paris, 1968), 81–88. G. Delling (*TWNT* 5:834, 1ff.) consistently interprets the Spirit's activity as an event of creation in the virgin birth.

8

Mary Magdalene and the Women at Jesus' Tomb

The following will be an attempt to describe how the Gospel of Mark views Mary Magdalene and the women at the tomb. Mark 15:40–16:8 is the oldest text known to us about women as disciples of Jesus. The view conveyed by the Gospel of Mark will then be compared with other views of the same situation in New Testament literature, especially with that of the Gospel of Matthew. Finally, the redaction-historical findings will be evaluated under two questions: First, which conclusions can we draw from them concerning the historical situation? Second, which conclusions can we draw from them concerning the situation of women in the Jesus movement?

The examination of the redaction-historical findings has to take into account primarily the literary and historical context of the entire Gospel. There is no doubt that Mark makes use of existing tradition in the passage we are considering. Yet even where tradition has been used in the Gospels, the particular piece of tradition takes on a certain meaning in the context of the overall text. For that reason, hypotheses on the form of the pre-Markan tradition are useful in discerning Markan ideas; what is more important for the understanding of the particular passage is its interpretation based on the existing literary context. The historical context for Mark 15:40–16:8 is the situation of a Gentile Christian community of faith outside Palestine shortly after 70 C.E.[1] To begin with, one will have to distinguish this historical context from the situation presented in Mark 15:40–16:8 at the time of Jesus' death in Jerusalem.

How Did Mark See It?

"But there were also women..." (15:40).[2] As can be seen from Mark 15:41, women followed Jesus already in Galilee. So far, they had not been mentioned. Now, Mark adds on the occasion of their role at the tomb that they had been around all along. The quasi-supplementary addition (15:41) is to make clear who the women at the cross of Jesus were; it is *not* intended to clarify the role of the women in Jesus' company in Galilee and on the way to Jerusalem. That is to say, Mark makes clear that so far he had been using the androcentric linguistic use common in antiquity, where women are included in the terminology that talks about men. He also makes clear that he is not critically predisposed toward this linguistic use. He shares this uncritical androcentric linguistic use with all other evangelists of the New Testament.

For example, Matthew wanted to increase the number of people in his stories on the feeding. For that reason, he says that there were five thousand (or four thousand) "men without [not counting] women and children" who were fed (Matt. 14:21; 15:38). Thereby, he shows that the Markan formulation of five thousand "men" in Mark 6:44 is normally understood in an inclusive fashion (also in Matt. 14:35). The fact that Mark means by the five thousand "men" both men and women is indirectly apparent from Matthew, but also from Mark 8:9, where only the number of those fed is given. This linguistic use, where women are included when only men are mentioned, can also be observed in other passages. When, according to Matt. 25:40, the most lowly of Jesus' "brothers" are destined to receive love offerings, certainly both men and women in need are meant. Also Luke uses this linguistic style; see Acts 1:15, 16, where the "men" include the women (mentioned in 1:14) of the early church in Jerusalem. If Luke intended not to include these women all of a sudden, he would have had to say so explicitly. Hence, one will have to assume for many passages of the Gospels that women are included by the evangelists when, for example, there is general talk about the "disciples," as in the address of the Sermon on the Mount or in the Sermon on the Plain (Matt. 5:1; Luke 6:20).

The curiosity of this androcentric linguistic use also becomes apparent when considering why women appear explicitly in the summary notes. They do not appear anywhere simply because the author thinks that he would be incomplete were he to name only men. Hence, there is no indication of the presence of a critical awareness concerning language that passes over women in silence. Instead, women are mentioned when one wants to express that there was a huge number of people (Acts 21:5—this verse makes clear that the *mathētai* of 21:4 includes also women and children; also Acts 5:14; 8:12, where the issue is the success of the mission). In Mark 15:40, women are mentioned because, according to Mark, only women were at the cross and near the tomb. In Acts 8:3 and 9:2, it is said that Paul acted as a persecutor of Christians with hatred and thoroughness; hence, it says explicitly: He persecuted men and women.³ While one cannot find a critical awareness of this androcentric language, Matthew and the Codex Cantabrigiensis make it their interest: They enter patriarchal conditions even in places where tradition does not have them.⁴

To Mark, the women at the cross of the dying Jesus were—as one can see from his linguistic use—among the disciples who fled when Jesus was arrested. He says explicitly that *all* fled, and he clarifies this situation still further by a narrative of the youth who, out of fear of being arrested, flees in the nude (Mark 14:50–52). Then, the fleeing disciples hid in Jerusalem. From this hiding place—that is at least the way Mark sees it—they emerged (as also Peter in 14:54) again, while the other disciples continued hiding.

"They looked on from a distance" (15:40). The crucifixion of people by Roman soldiers had grave consequences for their friends and relatives.⁵ Those crucified were to remain hanging on the cross for deterrence, until the animals would have eaten the bodies. The refusal of a burial was part of the sentence, which was intended to hurt especially friends and relatives. The amount of shame for the relatives resulting from the refusal of burial can be seen by the fact that the crucified bodies were often guarded by Roman soldiers to prevent the relatives from stealing the bodies.⁶ Whoever buried a body in spite of the burial prohibition was punished. Like the burial, also the act of mourning was forbidden. It is reported that many times people crying over the death of one crucified were crucified themselves. Tacitus writes about Tiberius's mass executions: "Neither relatives nor friends were allowed to come close, to weep for them, not even to look at them for a while longer. There were guards all around, who paid attention whether someone showed some sign of sadness."⁷ For the followers of Jesus, this situation may have been even more dangerous than for his relatives since the Romans considered Jesus' crucifixion a political

act. Attempting to bury the crucified, weeping for him, or showing any kind of behavior that would reveal one as a follower of Jesus could have been a dangerous act of solidarity that might have led to being crucified oneself. Josephus reports on mass crucifixions by the Roman governor Felix: "The number of thieves he crucified and of citizens who could be shown to have been associated with them and whom he henceforth punished, grew to be enormous."[8]

The behavior of the women in Mark 15:40–16:8, the behavior of the disciples in Mark 14:50–53, the behavior of Peter in Mark 14:54, 66–72, and the behavior of Joseph of Arimathea have to be viewed in light of the historical context described here.[9] In this case, the same historical context has to be assumed in order to understand both the situation during Jesus' death and the passion narrative in the Gospel of Mark (and in the other Gospel accounts of the New Testament), since the role of sentencing by crucifixion both in the Palestine of Jesus and in other areas of the Roman Empire did not change during the first century.[10]

When the text says that the women were looking at the cross "from a distance," one has the historical right to say: They tried to remain unidentified, even though they took a great risk.[11] The fact that they were women was, by the way, no protection; women and children also were crucified.[12] The walk to the tomb on Easter morning has to be viewed against this background also. J. Blinzler's assumption that the graves of executed political enemies of the Roman Empire were feared to become "pilgrims' sites of like-minded and hence ... a gathering spot of conspiring elements," describes the situation correctly.[13] Being found at Jesus' tomb involved a great risk, just as other activities did that revealed an affiliation with the one crucified.

A passage in Ps. 37:12 ("my neighbors stood far from me" [cf. Ps. 87:9]) may play a role in Mark 15:40 when Jesus' situation is described;[14] yet this is not to suggest that the passion narrative has been invented from biblical motives, but that a quite realistic—and also repeatable—event is being experienced as having been prophesied in the Bible. The fear of Jesus' followers who told this story about the women at the cross to one another in light also of their own experiences did not diminish when they said that the event was God's doing; but they experienced their fear as an element of a story of God's activity, the purpose of which was salvific.

"*Among them were also Mary of Magdala and Mary of James the Lesser(,) and the mother of Joses, and Salome*" *(15:40).* During the burial only two women are watching (15:47), and three go to the tomb on Easter morning (16:1), while here, at the crucifixion, there are many women watching. The fact that there are many women is mentioned twice (v. 40, *en hais;* v. 41, *kai allai pollai*); hence, it is important for the text. One will have to understand this information in the context of Mark 3:6–8. For Mark, the disciples are included in the fate of Jesus' passion,[15] for which reason he draws this concrete picture: After the decision to kill Jesus had been taken by a number of Jews, a crowd follows from Galilee and from other areas (3:6); many women from Galilee (and possibly other areas—on this see the discussion below on 15:41) are at the cross, having come there because they had become Jesus' disciples and walked along with him up to Jerusalem. The cross was the end of their way behind Jesus. In this scene, the women represent all of Jesus' disciples and their discipleship of the cross, which stands at the center of Mark's Gospel. Mark has neither a positive nor a negative view toward the fact that the disciples at the cross are exclusively women: It is not difficult for him to portray the women's discipleship of the cross as representative for all of Jesus' disciples, but he does not thereby intend to bestow on women, who are hardly esteemed, a special honor.[16]

At least in Mark's view, four (not three) women are mentioned.[17] Mary the wife (or daughter) of James the

Lesser stands at Jesus' cross (15:40–41) and is one of the three women going to the tomb on Easter morning (16:1). She has to be distinguished from Mary (15:47) the mother of Joses (15:40); the latter stands at the cross and later watches the burial (15:47). There is no reason for assigning the list of names in 15:40, 47 and 16:1 in tradition-historical manner to different traditions.[18] In the present context, they make sense and produce no contradictions, and the possibility of their origin in old Christian, pre-Markan tradition goes back less to tradition-historical than to social-historical considerations about the form of names: The male relatives in these women's lists are probably also followers of Jesus. After all, such names are supposed to make possible the distinguishing of persons (in this instance, of different women all by the name of Mary) by association with known persons. So these names are not formal names, as may be found primarily in letters of divorce, but names of association that have a "restricted range of association"[19] and presuppose a social group in which the named relatives are known. The men mentioned in the women's lists, James the Lesser and Joses, do not appear elsewhere in the New Testament.[20] That means, however, that the acquaintance with these two men was not passed on in written or oral tradition known to us—through "literary" reference, that is. It is highly possible, then, that these name-traditions go back to a rather early tradition, and that Mark passes them on faithfully because he probably no longer knows these people. Mark does not have the tendency here, occasionally observed elsewhere, of substituting unfamiliar names with names familiar to Christian literary tradition. Possibly for that reason, Salome is substituted in Matthew's account with the mother of the sons of Zebedee (Matt. 27:56). Matthew knows no longer what to do with the names of two Marys differentiated by their male relatives in Mark 15:40, 47 and 16:1; hence, he makes both out to be one person, the "other Mary," mother of James and Joseph (Matt. 27:56; 28:1).

The fact that the name-tradition in Mark 15:40 and other passages goes back to the oldest tradition is supported by the unusual[21] naming of a woman after her son (the mother of Joses). This name has to come from a group where this Joses, unknown to us from the New Testament, was so familiar that one even identified his mother by him.

Mary Magdalene does not have a male relative who is known to the Christian community; hence, she is identified by her place of origin.[22] This name of origin has "emerged abroad,"[23] and hence presupposes that Mary Magdalene no longer lived in Magdala. From her name alone and from her presence in Jerusalem after Jesus' death, one can conclude what the text is reporting: that she followed Jesus from Galilee to Jerusalem. Even if the entire text of Mark 15:40–16:8 were to be Markan in form and allowed hardly any assumptions of a pre-Markan tradition, the name Mary Magdalene in its connection with Jesus' tomb in Jerusalem corroborates, as such, the story narrated in 15:40ff.

Martin Hengel, primarily, has seen the sequence of names in Mark 15:40, 47 and 16:1 (and in the Synoptic parallels) as an ordering of rank, in which the special rank of Mary Magdalene is based on "her 'priority in the sequence of epiphanies and the story of the apostolic Easter message.' "[24] This ranking order, however, is viewed within the church as a matter of authority and prestige. Hengel even thinks that women standing at the cross "were fighting their female rivals" and that from that the differing names next to Mary Magdalene's can be explained. There were many people who followed Jesus, and they pressed their claims for prestige later in various ways.[25] The fact that Mary Magdalene is the only one who is always named in these lists—and always in first place—is indeed conspicuous and can be compared foremost with Peter's role within the lists of the disciples; one will have to agree with Hengel on that. Nevertheless, despite the many traces of arguments over rank in early Christian communities (see Mark 10:35–45 par.), tradition is quite aware, particularly in relation to this matter, that one cannot assume a ranking "as at banquets,"[26] and so on, within the churches. In addition, the text gives no evidence that women argued over rank. The fact that various women's names are mentioned next to Mary Magdalene's has to do with what the respective group who recites those names in its stories associates with these persons. Therefore, one should not imagine Mary Magdalene's authority in terms of rank within a hierarchically structured group, but in terms of authority, resulting from some task within the church. The naming of Mary Magdalene in first place shows that one knew how important her behavior was to the Jesus movement after Jesus' death. In that, she is to be compared with Peter. In addition, the Markan text, as also the parallels in Luke and Matthew, does not provide evidence that competition existed between the significance of Mary Magdalene and that of Peter (see below on 16:7).

"... *who, when he was in Galilee, followed and served him*" *(15:41).* One can assume that at least the four women mentioned by Mark walked with Jesus already in Galilee and, thereafter, followed him to Jerusalem. Their presence at the cross is a result of their discipleship, as was already shown. While the word *akolouthein* depicts the disciples' existence in general (see 1:18; 8:34; 10:28), the discipleship of women receives a special character in exegetical literature due to its connection with *diakonein:* The meaning of *diakonein* is filled in with reference either to Luke 8:3 or to Mark 1:31; in either case, the service of women is distinguished from the service of men through reference to Mark 15:41.[27] Hence, one assumes that either the women supported Jesus from their own funds or that they provided meals for him as Martha did (Luke 10:38–42), since Mark 1:31 is mostly interpreted in light of the view in Luke 10:38–42. Yet one cannot use Lukan texts right away for an interpretation; one has to ask first what the Gospel of Mark means by *dia-*

konia. The clearest interpretation of the word is in Mark 10:42–45 and 9:35. It denotes here the situation of one standing at the lowest level of social hierarchy (contrast *prōtos, megas* with *pantōn eschatos, diakonos, doulos*). In discipleship of Jesus, one does not strive to rise and rule over others, but precisely to remain lowly. "To be the servant and slave of all," hence, is an important part of discipleship of Jesus of whatever form; it means that within the congregation, domination of people over people cannot exist: All are *diakonoi* of all. Therefore, the term *diakonia* in the Gospel of Mark has a much more comprehensive meaning than only that of service at the table: It denotes the relationship of disciples among each other, their relationship to Jesus, and that of Jesus to the people (10:45). One can easily align the other uses of the word group *diakonia* in Mark with the clearly pronounced meaning of the term in 9:35 and 10:42–45. It is important to note, as E. Stegemann in particular has pointed out, that the verb is always in the imperfect (1:13, 31; 15:41),[28] so that even the choice of tense prohibits the limited interpretation in terms of table service: Should one, indeed, imagine that Peter's mother-in-law is serving Jesus and the disciples at the table on a permanent basis (1:31)?

Mark 1:31c does not depict a healing but the discipleship of the healed woman that resulted from the healing; for Mark it is part of discipleship that a healed person proclaims Jesus' works (1:45; 5:20; 10:52). The word *diakonia* can doubtlessly also denote table service, but with it are connected other aspects, too: the renunciation of wanting to be great and to rule, a renunciation that can be made concrete in many other ways—in receiving a child (9:36 after 9:35) and in Jesus' death (10:45). When in Mark 15:41 the *diakonia* of the women toward Jesus is mentioned in particular, the term is almost synonymous with *akolouthein*. The women serve Jesus also when they want to show him honor by embalming in the tomb. Mark 16:1 is an example of their *diakonia*. Yet *diakonia* is nothing especially typical for women. In regard to Mark

15:41, the common distinction between the service of women and the service of men does not have its origin in the New Testament itself but, rather, in a preunderstanding of exegetes. After all, the New Testament makes it completely clear—given what has been said about the Gospel of Mark—that the term *diakonia* is not associated with a specific role of women but with the situation of one who is all the way at the bottom and has to do the worst jobs. Table service as a lowly type of work is one form of *diakonia:* The slave experienced, mainly in the *diakonia*, his or her social situation in an especially dramatic way (see Luke 12:37; 17:8; 22:27)[29] because antiquity had rather strict hierarchical regulations for meals, where the server—slave, son or daughter, or wife—was always the socially lowest. Yet rather than being characteristic of the woman, even among the lowly, this serving role was more typical of the slave.[30] Perhaps one should translate *diakonein* as "being subject" in order to express what the New Testament, and with it Mark, associates with this term. The fact that this word signifies the relationship of every single person to any other person in early Christianity shows how hard the people in discipleship of Jesus tried to put into practice the eschatological reversal of all power structures among people (Matt. 20:16 par.; Luke 1:46–47).[31]

"...*and the many other women, who went up with him to Jerusalem*" *(15:41b).* In Mark 15:40, 41a, the discipleship of women in Galilee is mentioned; now, Mark 15:41b tells of how the group followed Jesus up to Jerusalem, and to the passion and resurrection, predicted by Jesus. The word *anabainein* denotes, besides the words *akolouthein* and *diakonein,* the journey of those following Jesus (10:32–34). For Mark, it is a journey leading to the confrontation with Jesus' death and also to a threat on the followers' own lives that filled them with fear (10:32). One might wonder whether Mark wants to enlarge the circle of women, mentioned in 15:40, by women following Jesus from regions other than Galilee (in light of 3:6–8, see above on *en hais* in 15:40). In any case, the word *synanabainein* includes the women from Galilee since, after all, the Galilean women stand at the cross in Jerusalem. The theological reason why Mark separates following Jesus within Galilee and *anabainein* to Jerusalem with such care—something in which Matthew (27:55) and Luke (23:49) do not follow him—is that the *anabainein* to the cross is to him of central importance in the discipleship of Jesus. The backdrop is the warranted fear of the Markan community of faith, which has such a prospect literally lying ahead[32] and which Mark wants to have the courage of faith. Also from this small phrase, one sees again that Mark views the women at the cross as representatives of the disciples and their discipleship of the cross. He is concerned with the discipleship of the cross; that only *women* are standing at the cross is something he makes nothing of.

"*Mary of Magdala, however, and the Mary of Joses saw where they laid him*" *(15:47)*. Two of the many women who had stood at the cross had witnessed, from a distance, the burial of Jesus in which they, however, did not participate. One commonly regards the "viewing" in Mark 15:47 as an eyewitnessing in a legal-theological sense, which relates to the women's eyewitness of Jesus' death (15:40) and the empty tomb (16:1–8).[33] Paul had left out again the witness of the women in 1 Cor. 15:3ff., supposedly because women could not be witnesses in Jewish jurisdiction.[34] However, the term "witness" with its legal connotation is not appropriate for interpreting the women's role here, and neither in Mark 15:40–16:8 in general, because nothing in Mark points to such an understanding. Also Luke, for whom the term *martys* (witness) is of central significance and for whom the women should have met the conditions (Acts 1:8, 21–22) of being witnesses of the resurrection, does not call them such; likewise, Luke does not interpret "being a witness" in a legal sense and the resurrection as a fact that can be separated from faith.[35]

Even if, according to the opinion of interpreters, the testimony of women is supposed to have its meaning in a larger sense (that it would be understood as a testimony against suspicions in the mind of the public—in other words, not in a legal but in an apologetic sense), there still is no evidence in the text for such a view. In addition, one has to take always into account that in the world of early Christianity the idea of the dead rising in a miraculous way did not constitute a rational contradiction (as it does for most people in our Enlightenment-oriented, scientific world of thinking) that would require witnesses' affidavits to resolve.[36] In any case, one may regard the women as witnesses in the sense that they proclaim the resurrection message. Their goal is to spark faith. The faith they seek to enkindle, however, is not only a faith in the limited sense of believing the fact of the resurrection: They are witnesses of a faith also in the full sense and, as such, are witnesses of the death and resurrection of Jesus, even though no evangelist calls them that.

Therefore, the point of 15:47 is not to note the women's eyewitness. In light of the reasons causing the women to look at the crucifixion only from afar (see above), one will have to understand what is said in 15:47 in its historical context, also: They cannot risk participating in the burial and showing signs of mourning; they can only go near the tomb after the burial.[37] The distance between them and Joseph of Arimathea is understandable when considering the danger involved for all. Hence, Mark 15:47 fits consistently in the narrative context and presupposes the continuation of events in 16:1–8.

"And when the Sabbath was over, Mary Magdalene and the Mary of James, and Salome bought ointments to go and embalm him" (16:1). One may assume that the timing reported here and in 16:2 has a symbolic secondary meaning,[38] yet one should not overlook that it makes very good sense in the reported sequence of events: The women wait until dusk, when the Sabbath is over and the spice shops in Jerusalem are open again. They buy aromatic oils and go,

at the first possible moment ("very early," "when the sun rose"), to the tomb. The implied importance of the time factor is to point out the loving kindness of their action: They came as fast as possible. The twofold reporting of timing in verse 2 renders this importance in a natural fashion and need not be understood as the result of an unbalanced process in tradition.

Now, the women intend to sprinkle aromatic oil on Jesus' body; thus, they want to honor the dead and show their loyalty to him. One will have to picture this situation: If they had been met by informers on Easter morning at the tomb, it could have cost them their lives (see above on 15:40).

The women's intention to embalm the body is commonly declared as foolish; after all, the body had been wrapped and, most of all, one could no longer embalm a body after two nights and one day in the Oriental climate.[39] Yet these assumptions are incorrect since the *aleiphein* here does not mean that the body was embalmed from head to toe as after a bath or after the washing of a dead person. Instead, *aleiphein* (embalming) has to be understood as a sprinkling of head or feet, an act of paying homage as Jesus has received it in Bethany from a woman (Mark 14:3). In 14:8, Jesus interprets this act of showing honor as an embalming of a body for burial. In light of antiquity's customs, we need to distinguish in this context between several kinds of embalming. One embalms the head in order to honor the person; a host, for example, embalms the guest.[40] One washes the body after death and before it is placed in the coffin or buried without coffin.[41] One sprinkles the aromatic oil on the body and places aromatic essences next to the body in order to honor the dead person.[42] It is this last act of honoring the dead that Mark 16:1 (also John 19:39 and Mark 14:8) is describing. In antiquity, not only the rich went through unreasonable expenses when it came to the use of aromatic oils and other aromatic substances. Both Mark 14:3 and John 12:3ff. convey a truthful picture of the value of the aromatic substance used and of how things were overdone: The poor Jesus is honored with oil of nard, one of the finest products among antiquity's luxury items.[43]

The women at Jesus' tomb did not buy nard; yet one has to consider that the aromatic oils they bought were certainly not cheap and were way beyond their income levels. But that is the oddity about honoring someone with aromatic substances in antiquity.

Therefore, the picture the Gospel of Mark conveys of Jesus' burial is without contradictions in itself and corresponds with what was common in antiquity. The burial through Joseph of Arimathea is not incomplete; neither is it viewed as such by the women.[44] Also, the women's walk to the tomb need not be viewed as an event that can be explained from a literary perspective so that, for example, the narrator has "an interest in the women's coming to the tomb at the earliest possible time after the end of the Sabbath rest" and, therefore, "needs to mention a reason that makes good sense."[45]

"Who will move the stone for us?" (16:3). In the same way, one should not isolate the scene in Mark 16:3–4 on the literary and religio-historical levels. Else, one says, for example, that verse 3 is hardly imaginable in reality since the women would have had to remember that they themselves could not get into the tomb;[46] it is "not appropriate wanting to look for historical events behind kerygmatic motives"—this phrase by H. Grass captures well a research consensus quite common even to this day.[47] But one does have to ask about the historical reality, both of what Mark had in mind and of what we can reconstruct from it about the events surrounding Jesus' death. Thereby, one does not intend to ignore the structure of the text and the religio-historical context. One's only purpose is to show that these considerations cannot be separated from the historical question. It is certainly true that the question in verse 3 prepares for the miracle, but the question also realistically describes the situation of the women who cannot expect any help, neither from the dis-

ciples nor from those walking by, of whom they should rather be afraid. The women do not pay a "normal" visit at a grave; they are going to the grave of one who was crucified. They want to honor the dead person, although they are faced with great difficulties: They are not supposed to attract attention. The women are not portrayed as forgetful but as tough and persistent in their affectionate desire. It is possible that the relatives may, in similar fashion, not have had a ladder and yet still reached the cross. (In *Satyricon* [111], Petronius refers to the relatives taking a dead person down from the cross in order to bury him, while the soldier on guard permitted himself a love adventure in a tomb nearby.)

"*They saw a young man*" *(16:5).* The wonderful encounter of the women means seeing (*eidon* in v. 5; *anablepsasai theōrousin* in v. 4; *ide* in v. 6), the hearing of the angel's message, and being frightened (*exethambēthēsan* in v. 5; cf. v. 6; *tromos kai ekstasis, ephobounto* in v. 8). The main point is that the women now act; the wonderful appearance is to change their lives (*hypagete; eipate* in v. 7). From a form-historical viewpoint, the women experience an epiphany. At its center is the angel's speech of revelation to the women, which dismisses the women with a concrete order. In this epiphany story, the women are the protagonists; it is about them, about a change in them, just as Acts 9:1–19 is about Paul and the change in him. The women are told of Jesus' resurrection during the angel's revelation, yet Mark 16:1–8 presupposes Jesus' resurrection and does not greatly concentrate on it. Jesus has risen earlier; he himself has rolled the stone away, or perhaps the stone rolled away by itself. He is no longer in the tomb where he was buried. The risen one is already on his way to Galilee (*proagei* in v. 7, but *proaxei* in 14:28), and the eschatological gathering has begun. Jesus' resurrection is not discussed as such; only the aspect of what its consequences are for the women and, hence, for all disciples.

By categorizing this passage as a narrative of an epiphany to the women, one brings about, primarily in respect to older research such as that represented by Rudolf Bultmann, two decisive changes. First, the text is perceived as a unit, meaningfully complete within itself, and does not contain the tension that would allow for a literary-critical assessment such as the following: According to Bultmann, verse 7 and verse 8 belong to two different literary strata.[48] Contrary to such an assessment, these verses are seen to form a meaningful unit in the context of Mark (see below). The pre-Markan tradition cannot be extrapolated by saying one observes tensions in the present text. Second, by viewing the passage as a unit, then, the function of the so-called empty tomb in this story also changes: The women fail before the angel's command (v. 7) and, though only indirectly, also before the message that Jesus is risen.

For the religio-historical discussion,[49] which shall be mentioned only briefly here, the idea of an assumption (*aphanismos*) into heaven is, in my view, no sufficient explanation for Mark 16:1–8, because Jesus is, according to Mark 16:1–8, not in heaven but rather is physically alive and on his way to Galilee. His resurrection has to be understood in the religio-historical aspect primarily from the context of apocalyptic hopes (see especially v. 7, discussed below). However, it is methodologically important that the meaning of singular characteristics, such as the fear of the women for example, has to be determined from the context first and can be compared only then to religio-historical material. All of the many epiphany narratives within and outside the Bible have their own respective meanings, and also the regularly mentioned fear on the part of those experiencing the epiphanies can have very different meanings.

"*He is risen, he is not here*" *(16:6)*. You are looking for the crucified, the angel tells the women. In these words, the angel sums up how the women have been acting since Jesus' death. They had been looking for his tomb, his body, to honor the dead person. That was the wrong kind of behavior. Jesus had told his disciples three times that he would have to suffer and that he would rise after three days (Mark 8:31; 9:31; 10:34). He had told them that the disciples would be a scattered flock (14:28). "You are looking... for the crucified"—you did not "remember" Jesus' prophesies (in the sense of 8:18); their hearts were hardened; they did not come to their senses yet: You have eyes and see not (8:17–20). They were looking for the body in the tomb, but should have, instead, been looking for the risen one by following him to Galilee.

The passage in Mark 16:1–8 is a last account of the disciples' failure, which is of great importance in the Gospel of Mark. Out of fear, Peter has denied his affiliation with Jesus, and now that Jesus has already risen, the disciples are still sitting in their hideout in Jerusalem; and, although these three women behave lovingly and courageously, they act in a totally wrong way. They lack *pistis;* else, they would know that Jesus is risen and that they have to take action again. The acknowledgment of the "empty tomb" does not serve as a demonstration of the resurrection,[50] but as a reproach to the women. They had been looking for Jesus in the wrong spot. Luke has expressed the idea of Mark 16:6 correctly: "Why are you looking for the living among the dead?... Remember what he told you" (Luke 24:5–6). The reason for the women's incorrect behavior becomes clear in the context: They are afraid just like Peter and just like the other disciples in the Gospel of Mark are again and again, and their fear is justified (see above on 15:40).

When the women are frightened by the appearance of the angel, it is, speaking in the technical sense of history of religion, a fright "typical" of recipients of revelation; the angel responds in the typical "comfort formula": "Do not be afraid." Yet the "numinous" fear here has its special characteristic: Both the women and the disciples have been the "scattered flock" since Jesus' arrest (14:27; Zech. 13:7). The angel has to pull them out of *this* condition. The women's fear of the angel also recalls again the reality of the disciples' fear (hence, the fear of the Markan community of faith). Especially verse 8 shows that one cannot separate here the fear of the divine appearance from the fear of impending persecution.

"*But go there, say...* " *(16:7)*. With this phrase, the decisive change takes place (*alla*, but): The angel's revelation is to change the women. People acting wrongly out of fear are to become people who, together with others, again follow Jesus; the scattered flock is to become again the gathered flock,[51] whom the shepherd precedes. Verse 7, then, is a command to the women. They are to tell the disciples and Peter that the risen one is preceding them on their journey to Galilee. This message for the disciples, however, is formulated in such a way as to address the women also: The plural form, used three times in the second person, addresses the women here already—and is, equally, an indication of what they are to tell the disciples. If the women were only to be "letter carriers," the text would have to use indirect speech or make clear in some other way that the women were not included. Yet not only the linguistic form includes the women in the Galilean prophesy of verse 7; also, and primarily, the connection with verse 6 makes clear that the promise of *opsesthe* is meant for them as well as for the disciples. They had been looking for Jesus in the wrong place. The angel directs them to the right place: There, you will find him, whom you no longer can see here in the tomb.

People have repeatedly contrasted the appearance of the angel to the women with the appearance of the risen one to Peter and the other disciples in terms of their content: The limited command to the women in Mark 16:7 (as also in the Christophany of Matt. 28:8–19) was considered of only preliminary importance. The women were no true resurrection witnesses (R. Pesch speaks of "primary witnesses"); Mark 16:7 implies that only "the disciples and Peter"—or the "Eleven," according to Matt. 28:16–20—were the true witnesses. (The same holds true for Luke and 1 Cor. 15:3ff.)[52] In Mark's (as also in Matthew's and Luke's) sense, this contrasting is only half correct. "Primary witnesses" are, indeed, those who see the risen one. In Mark 16:1–8, the women receive, indeed, a limited command. Yet also to them (16:7) the angel proclaims that they will see the risen one, just as Jesus' prophecy in 14:28 was meant also for them. The groups among the disciples are not explicitly distinguished against each other. The prophesy in 14:28 is directed to the Twelve (14:17); and 16:7 renews and concretizes (*opsesthe*) this prophesy to the "disciples and to Peter." At the same time, the three women mentioned in 16:1 are addressed also. In my view, the "Twelve" of the Gospel of Mark are representatives of the "disciples," which include also the women. Peter, on his part, also occasionally represents the "Twelve."

"They did not tell anyone about it, since they were afraid" (16:8). The flight of the women from the tomb in spite of Jesus' resurrection, in spite of the angel's revelation, is probably the gravest failure of the disciples in the Gospel of Mark—and on top of everything else, it comes at the end of the text. The flight of the disciples (14:50) is, even at this point, not over yet. It is continued by the three women. So the Gospel of Mark ends by describing how the disciples, as a scattered flock, sit in their hideouts in Jerusalem. Also the women hide again and refuse, out of fear, to carry out the order. Jesus is risen, and his disciples are unable to see him. The power of fear has conquered faith.[53] The Gospel of Mark implicitly presupposes that the great failure of Peter, of the women, as well as of the disciples in general is not the final word about Jesus' disciples. Implicitly, Peter is the central carrier of Jesus' message, even though the last thing Mark's Gospel reports on him is his failure (14:66–72). The Gospel of Mark presupposes that its readers and hearers know that the women ultimately have carried out the order, that Jesus appeared to the disciples in Galilee, and that he commissioned them anew with spreading the message (see 13:10). It is foretold that the cowardly

Peter and the frightened Mary Magdalene will become witnesses of the resurrection, role models of a fear overcome. Why, then, does the Gospel of Mark still end on a negative note?

The reason for that is, in my view, primarily the actual situation of the Markan community (or communities) of faith. This community experiences the situation of a scattered flock, that of Peter who denies Jesus, that of the women who flee from the tomb. Mark does not want to speak at that time of the gathering of the flock with Jesus in the lead because the flock he sees is scattered. The positive continuation of the desperate last sentence in Mark 16:8 can be acted out only by the community.[54] This action of the community can be concretely identified. Peter's risk when acknowledging his discipleship has remained timely throughout the entire first century and beyond. The situation of Mark's community is such that through the pressure of persecution,[55] its entire future existence is questioned. Romans were suspicious of any form of cooperation among people; they suspected "rebellion" very quickly. Nevertheless, Jesus' followers are to enter upon the road of discipleship, then during Jesus' time as well as now during Mark's, and they are to draw their own conclusions from Jesus' resurrection.[56] One can identify the existing dilemma if one looks at Mark 16:8 in connection with Mark 14:27 and Mark 4:17; the word *skandalizesthai* summarizes the situation described in Mark 16:8. Only the practice of faith can lead out of this dilemma, yet it involves massive danger. Although the promise of Mark 10:28–30 applies to the community, it applies "while under persecution" (10:30). The gathering of the scattered in the existing community is seen in an eschatological fashion. The community is the head of a bridge to the longed-for near and ultimate gathering of the chosen ones, coming from all corners of the world, when the Son of man appears (13:26–27). One does not do justice to this eschatology by interpreting the "seeing" of the risen one in Galilee *either* as the parousia *or* as an epiphany in the sense of 1 Cor. 15:3ff. since to Mark, both aspects are closely related. Jesus' resurrection is the decisive, world-changing, eschatological event—a beginning that soon will lead up to the ultimate goal, the appearance of the Son of man in the clouds. Faith's task is to point out through the promises in scripture and those made by Jesus what needs to be done *now*.

Mark 15:40–16:8 and Matthew 27:55–28:20

When comparing the Markan report concerning Mary Magdalene and the women at the tomb with that of Matthew, the similarity between the two reports is impressive, even though the theological emphases differ. Although Matthew's community lives under the pressure of persecution as well (see 24:9–14), the particularity in which Mark expresses people's fears and in which he wants to enable them to act is not adopted by Matthew. In Matthew, the women carry out the angel's order (28:8), and an appearance to the Eleven on a mount in Galilee is reported (28:16–20).

For Matthew, the appearance to the Eleven is probably not one to all followers including women; he does not even imply the inclusion of women. After all, he has changed the form of *opsesthe* in 28:10, which also in his Gospel (28:7) includes the women; the followers will see him (*opsontai*). However, the content of the women's message to the disciples is of greater weight in Matthew than in Mark: They are to say what the angel ordered them to say (28:7), namely, *ēgerthē apo tōn nekrōn ... proagei*. ... This message of the angel is made even more concrete during a Christophany (28:8–10). Now, the women are to bring word about an immediate departure, *hina apelthōsin* (28:10).[57]

Within the context, the meaning of these two orders of proclamation is the following: The disciples have fled (26:56). Peter has denied Jesus out of (justified) fear (26:69ff.). Only the women look on the cross from a distance (27:55). Jesus, however, had foretold the flight of the disciples and the denial of Peter (26:31–35; cf. 26:75) and had interpreted both flight and denial as the scattering of the sheep, to be followed by their gathering (26:32). This eschatological gathering, foretold by Jesus, is the central theme of 28:1–20. The angel foretold the gathering on his part also (28:7) with the emphasized addition of *idou eipon hymin*. That means, on the one hand: What I am saying is a prophetic announcement, which you will remember; on the other hand, the importance and the "self-confidence"[58] of this messenger of God are emphasized. He is not an *angelus interpres* but a messenger of God who speaks with authority. The appearance of the risen one to the women constitutes a new event with its own meaning: Jesus orders (see *etaxato* in 28:16) that the disciples now depart. Matthew 28:1–7 and 28:8–10 prepare for 28:16–20.[59]

Although clearly Matthew thinks more patriarchally than Mark and Luke (see above on Mark 15:40 and, for example, the role of Mary in the birth narrative of Matthew), he has no problem in portraying the women here in an important role: They proclaim the resurrection to the disciples with divine authority (28:7) and initiate, upon Jesus' command, the eschatological course of events (28:10). They are portrayed as true believers who worship Jesus (28:8; see 14:33) and proclaim the message of salvation upon divine command (28:7).[60] Their message is not to elevate the credibility of the disciples' message but stands parallel to theirs. That Christ is risen states everything that is then spoken of in 28:16–20: He is the Lord of the whole world and, as the risen one, is present as "God with us" (1:23; 18:20; 28:20). What matters in 28:1–8 and 28:16–20 is not the credibility of the resurrection in an apologetic sense. What matters is the central content of the Christian proclamation. The term *ēgerthē* is an abbreviated version of what the risen one says at length in 28:16–20.

In Matthew, as in Mark, the appearance of the angel (28:1–8) has to be regarded as an epiphany story whose central point is the commissioning of the women by means of revelation. Matthew, however, imagines the situation a little differently from and clearly more concretely than Mark in that this event is one belonging to the beginning of end times.[61] The two women come to the tomb in the morning only to look at it, because it is sealed up and guarded. All of a sudden, the messenger of God appears, the earth trembles (28:2; cf. the apocalyptic happening in 27:51–53), and the angel moves away the stone. He sits down on it as on a throne and, from there, addresses the women, who do not enter the tomb itself (see also *apelthousai* in 28:8), despite the angel's invitation (28:6).

Historical Conclusions Concerning the Situation at the Time of Jesus' Death

Both Mark and Matthew presuppose that it is women who, after leaving the tomb, find the way to the risen one. Both seem to have little interest that they are women. There is hardly any other way of explaining this fact, in my opinion, than to assume that an old tradition reports such an activity on the women's part after Jesus' death. Therefore, and also because of the name list in the Markan tradition (see above on Mark 15:40), one can conclude that the relevant formulations of Mark 15:40–16:8 come from a pre-Markan tradition: Mary Magdalene and some other women from Galilee, who were among Jesus' followers from the very start, have been commissioned after Jesus' death by divine revelation to gather the crowd of followers, dispelled due to Jesus' crucifixion. The actual restoration of the coherence among Jesus' followers is connected with an epiphany of the risen one in Galilee to, naturally, all those who were still ready to carry on Jesus' message. If one tries to image the situation, it becomes self-evident that the women who had again taken initiative were present. There is no reason for doubting that the basic information provided by pre-Markan tradition (which cannot be proven by textual reconstructions) matches the historical situation during the time of Jesus' death. Matthew did not change these important basic facts of the tradition. The reason for the tradition's continuity is primarily that Jesus' followers who lived during the time Jesus died and Jesus' followers who lived during Mark's and Matthew's times were, historically speaking, in the same situation: Following the crucified one meant one's life was threatened by the Roman government. The crucial point, then, was the community's inner coherence, both after Jesus' death and in Mark's and Matthew's times. A scattered flock would no longer have been persecuted by the Romans; but a community of Jesus' followers, headed by the risen one, would.

Historical Inferences from the Situation of the Women During the Jesus Movement

One can conclude from what has been said that a group of Galilean women took, after Jesus' death in Jerusalem, decisive steps that lead to the restoration of the Galilean Jesus movement that had dissolved with Jesus' crucifixion. Hence, these women were the first among Jesus' disciples who believed Jesus' prophesy about the resurrection, even though it took the epiphany of an angel to confront them anew with the truth of Jesus' promise.[62] The obstacles they had to overcome were quite obviously given in the power politics Rome exercised in the occupied provinces. One will have to distinguish between the historical significance of the Galilean women, inferred from the texts, and the opinion of those who reported these happenings. One should note that the reporters in no way tried to retouch these happenings, that is, to reduce the women's role. Also, these events were not viewed as secondary compared to the Christophany in Galilee. Not even the Gospel of Luke, which tells the story differently, shows traces of an interest in reducing the women's importance. The fact that the disciples did not believe the women's report and regarded it as women's prattle (Luke 24:11) does not mean to Luke that the women were not believed because they were women (as is often interpreted). The disciples did not believe the *content* of the women's words because they could not believe that the crucified one was the Messiah (see 24:21, 25–27). With Jesus' death, the women experience the same paralysis as the disciples; they do not "remember" Jesus' prophecy (24:6). Luke also agrees with Mark and Matthew that neither the women nor the disciples in general are to be made heroes. The underlying reason for this quite relaxed and altogether nonpatriarchal reporting about the role of women is the practice of the Christian communities of the first century. The women were, as we also know from Paul, partakers in the prophetic proclamation of the gospel.

Nevertheless, the paradox remains that despite the practice of equality, which can be inferred from Mark 16:1–8 and Matt. 28:1–20, a more or less appropriate theoretical reflection of the women's role in the communities is missing. The language of all the Synoptic Gospels (including that of the Gospel of Luke) is androcentric. Even though one finds a theoretical reflection of the women's role in Mark 10:2–9 and in Luke 10:38–42 and 11:27–28,[63] these texts are only weak voices compared to the forcefulness of androcentric language and the absence of definite advocacy concerning the equality of the sexes. This contradiction between theory and practice in regard to women, also apparent in Paul, can perhaps be explained by the fact that the church was a minority and under persecution.[64] Unfortunately, for centuries to come, this contradiction had negative consequences for the situation of women in the church, though the church's situation was now changed.

Notes

1. On the historical placing and the redaction-historical method, see L. Schottroff, "Die Gegenwart in der Apokalyptik der synoptischen Evangelien," in *Befreiungserfahrungen: Studien zur Sozialgeschichte des Neuen Testaments* (Munich, 1990), 73–95.

2. Biblical quotations in this chapter are translated directly from the author's German.—ED.

3. It certainly is historically correct to say that women also were persecuted. The point here is, however, to find out why this fact is stated.

4. *Anthrōpos* in Matt. 19:5 means husband, in Mark 10:7, 9 (see also 10, 11ff.) man and woman; in Matt. 14:21 and 15:38, only men are counted. Concerning this, one has to point particularly to Acts 1:14, where Codex D makes the women of the early church in Jerusalem—the women as disciples of Jesus since Galilee (Luke 8:1–3) and at Jesus' tomb (Luke 23:49ff.)—to be the "women and children" of the apostles; see on that mainly W. Thiele, "Eine Bemerkung zur Apg. 1,14," *ZNW* 53 (1962): 110–11. On the androcentric language of the New Testament, see E. Schüssler Fiorenza, "Der Beitrag der Frau zur urchristlichen Bewegung," in W. Schottroff and W. Stegemann, eds., *Traditionen der Befreiung 2* (Munich, 1980), 60–90; here 67ff.

5. "Friends and relatives" are explicitly mentioned in this context by Philo, *In Flaccum* 72, and Tacitus, *Ann.* 6.19. In most pertinent documents, usually only the relatives are mentioned.

6. Petronius, *Satyricon* 111, and Eusebius, *Church History* 5.1.61; see also the numerous texts referring to exceptions when a body was released and permission given to bury it. These texts presuppose the guarding of the body; see a col-

lection of materials in J. Blinzler, *Der Prozess Jesu*, 4th ed. (Regensburg, 1969), 385–94.

7. Tacitus, *Ann.* 6.19; see also 6.10. On the prohibition of mourning, see also Suetonius, *Tiberius* 61; *Digestae* 3.2.11.3; Philo, *In Flaccum* 72.

8. Josephus, *BJ* 2.253.

9. Joseph of Arimathea could only "dare" doing so, since he himself was—as the text also tells—an influential personality (Mark 15:43). His "daring" deed was his demonstrated solidarity with the crucified. Jesus' disciples—men or women— were, in contrast to Joseph of Arimathea, lowly, insignificant people. Joseph of Arimathea's courageous step should not be seen as one where he "could dare approach the Roman governor *directly*...in contrast to the many women"; so G. Fitzer, in *TWNT* 8:185/2ff. (emphasis added).

10. For information on the crucifixion, see especially M. Hengel, "Mors turpissima crucis," in *Rechtfertigung* (Tübingen, 1976), 125–84.

11. Mark 15:54 describes this very situation with the same phrase.

12. Josephus, *BJ* 2.307.

13. Blinzler, *Prozess*, 386 n. 14.

14. See, for example, E. Klostermann, *Das Markusevangelium*, HNT 3, 4th ed. (Tübingen, 1950), 168. Concerning Mark 14:54 and 15:40, R. Pesch (*Das Markusevangelium*, HTKNT 2 [Freiburg, 1977], vol. 2) takes into account—apart from the biblical theme of the *passio iusti* traditions—the importance of the concrete historical situation. However, he interprets the note that the women watch "from afar" in this historical sense: "The fact that they are watching 'from afar' corresponds with the common behavior of women who live in a male-dominated, cruel world" (p. 505). This notion makes the reality of women much more innocuous than it really was.

15. On the interpretation of Mark 3:6–8, see especially E. Stegemann, "Das Markusevangelium als Ruf in die Nachfolge" (Diss., University of Heidelberg, 1974), 132. J. Schreiber (*Theologie des Vertrauens* [Hamburg, 1967], 174) points to the connection between Mark 15:40ff. and Mark 3:7ff.

16. J. Schniewind, *Das Evangeliums nach Markus*, NTD 1, 5th ed. (Göttingen, 1949), 202. He says: "Perhaps it is told on purpose that, while the disciples flee, the women stay on; the same

happens in 14:6–9 with the anointing woman, who understands Jesus' walk into death, while the disciples reproach her (14:3–5). It is clear that Jesus bestows honor on the woman, as he bestows honor on all those who are otherwise despised and lowly." I can agree with him when, subsequently, he points to a *practice* of the first Christian community, where the social rank of men and women seems to have been dissolved; however, I do not feel that the Gospel of Mark with the above-cited passage provides this insight; missing in Mark (as in all other Gospels) is an explicit remark on women analogous to Mark 2:15ff.; 10:13ff. In Mark 14:3ff. and in 15:40ff., disciples and women are *not contrasted*. Instead, the women repeat the failure of the disciples once again (16:8); they are ignorant and frightened like the male disciples. Additionally, the use of the word "disciples" not meaning men only speaks against Schniewind's assessment.

17. The Codex Vaticanus has also interpreted this easily misunderstood text in this way by means of adding a definite article. Here and in the following, the interesting name-tradition of this passage cannot be discussed for reasons of space. I presuppose the text-critical conclusions coming from the twenty-sixth edition of Nestle-Aland.

18. One can only point to the quite elaborate history of research on this question; see Pesch, *Das Markusevangelium*, 505ff. or J. Blinzler, *Die Brüder und Schwestern Jesu*, SBS 21 (Stuttgart, 1967). Blinzler (p. 83) argues that in 15:40 Mark means to speak of three women; his most important argument is that a topical continuation exists between 15:47 and 16:1; hence, the Mary of Joses (15:47) and the Mary of James are one and the same. Yet this argument is not pressing: After all, the presence of Salome (16:1) shows that the group's continuity is not of interest to the text; also, it would be rather odd to give the same woman two different names.

19. L. Köhler, "Die Personalien des Oktateuchs," *ZAW* 40 (1922): 34.

20. Joses is not identical with the Joses mentioned in Mark 6:3; see, for example, Pesch (*Das Markusevangelium*) on Mark 6:3; 15:40.

21. Such naming, for example, does not appear in the Octateuch, evaluated by L. Köhler, "Die Personalien."

22. One can presume that she has no family and no husband; at any rate, she lives within the group of Jesus' followers without relatives. But one cannot show from the text that she remained single (Pesch, *Das Markusevangelium*, 505) because of her grave disease of seven demons, of which Luke 8:2 reports; such an assumption is just as fantastic as the later Christian evolvement of legends that identify her with the sinner in Luke 7:37.

23. Köhler, "Die Personalien," 35 (on Typus 22).

24. M. Hengel, "Maria Magdalena und die Frauen als Zeugen," in *Abraham unser Vater* (Tübingen, 1963), 251; Hengel's quote is from E. Stauffer, *Jesus: Gestalt und Geschichte* (Bern, 1957), 114, with whom Hengel agrees.

25. Hengel, "Maria Magdalena," 247–48.

26. Ibid., 250.

27. Ibid., 248: "Through this service of women, they were to be freed from providing for the bodily well-being... of Jesus and his disciples for the service of proclaiming the prophesies of the impending Kingdom of God"; perhaps an intermediate step to the later diaconate office was to be made visible. Hengel interprets Mark 15:41 through Luke 8:3; Pesch (*Das Markusevangelium*, on that passage) and W. Beyer (*TWNT* 2:85) do the same. On Mark 1:31, E. Schweizer (*Das Evangelium nach Markus*, NTD 1 [Göttingen, 1967]) uses the phrase "specific form of a woman's discipleship"; Jesus displayed greater liberality than the rabbis, "who scorned at women's serving at the table." On this last comment, which is historically incorrect and is based on a generalization by Billerbeck, see E. Stegemann, *Das Markusevangelium*, 110. Unfortunately, such generalizations based on the comments of individual rabbis from later centuries have been employed again and again in relation to the problem of women as disciples of Jesus in order to establish a contrast between Jesus and Judaism, which does not stand up to historical examination. Such a wrong picture in this respect has been drawn primarily by Billerbeck and by J. Leipoldt, *Jesus und die Frauen* (Leipzig, 1921), but also by A. Oepke in "Gynē," *TWNT* 1, esp. 781–85. One can only point to this problem here; see on that also chap. 4, above.

28. E. Stegemann, *Das Markusevangelium*, 104, 111–12; and L. Schenke, *Die Wundererzählungen des Markusevangeliums* (Stuttgart, 1974), 111; Schenke correctly understands, in ref-

erence to Mark 9:35 and 10:43, 45, the service of Peter's mother-in-law as a "role model of true discipleship."

29. One cannot discuss here further material on the *diakonia* of the New Testament. One does not find in Paul a technical use of the word yet. All *charismata* are *diakoniai* in certain respects (1 Cor. 12:4).

30. See on that especially S. Krauss, *Talmudische Archäologie*, 3:46–50; J. Marquardt, *Das Privatleben der Römer* (Leipzig, 1886), 1:57, 146–47.

31. See on that L. Schottroff and W. Stegemann, *Jesus and the Hope of the Poor* (Maryknoll, N.Y.: Orbis Books, 1986).

32. See on that L. Schottroff, "Die Gegenwart." The women of 15:41b cannot be distinguished from the women in 15:40, 41a due to the importance of *anabainein*. Pesch (*Das Markusevangelium*, 508) suggests that the women are "not to be addressed equally as his [Jesus'] followers," but that is incorrect. Also, the women are not a new, third group of believers (the centurion, the women in vv. 40, 41a, the women in v. 41b) that could be contrasted with a third of three mocking groups during the crucifixion (W. Schenk, "Die gnostisierende Deutung des Todes Jesu und ihre kritische Interpretation durch den Evangelisten Markus," in W. Tröger, ed., *Gnosis und Neues Testament* [Gütersloh, 1973], 243).

33. Hengel, "Maria Magdalena," 256. He views the "eyewitness of women at the cross, at the burial, and at the empty tomb" as the central content of the tradition of women. He interprets the term "witness" on the one hand legally (pp. 246–47) and on the other in a theological-kerygmatic way, primarily so because he maintains the historicity of Mary Magdalene's being the first one to see the risen one and "the first to bring the message of the master's resurrection to the disciples" (p. 256). The legal aspect of the eyewitness is interpreted in very concrete fashion by Blinzler, *Prozess*, 402–3; he assumes that the two women (together with Joseph of Arimathea, since women's testimonies are not considered valid among Jews) are "witnesses of the historicity of the burial and of the exact situation of the tomb." Concerning 15:47, Pesch calls them "witnesses," but then criticizes (*Das Markusevangelium*, 538) a legal interpretation of this role in light of 16:1–8; see also H. von Campenhausen, *Der Ablauf der Osterereignisse und das leere Grab*, Sitzungsbericht der Heidelberger Akademie der Wis-

senschaften, Philos.-hist. Klasse, 3d ed. (Heidelberg, 1966), 41.

34. Hengel, "Maria Magdalena," 246.

35. C. Burchard, *Der dreizehnte Zeuge* (Göttingen, 1970), 133.

36. Referring to Mark 6:14–16 may be enough here.

37. Such is the reasonable assumption by Pesch (*Das Markusevangelium*, 517) due to the verb tenses. It has been assumed continually that 15:47 is secondary in the context, on the one hand, because of the difference in the name lists, and, on the other hand, due to the loose connection with the burial. Both arguments are not compelling. On the newer discussion for these arguments, see J. Broer, *Die Urgemeinde und das Grab Jesu* (Munich, 1972), 113ff.

38. This symbolic meaning is especially emphasized by Schreiber, *Theologie des Vertrauens*, 100–102.

39. J. Wellhausen, *Das Evangelium Marci*, 2d ed. (Berlin, 1909), 135; Pesch, *Das Markusevangelium*, 529; more literature in Schenke, *Die Wundererzählungen*, 31.

40. On the anointing with aromatic oil for honoring the living, see Luke 7:36–50; Ps. 23:5; E. Kutsch, *Salbung als Rechtsakt* (Berlin, 1963), 5; Krauss, *Talmudische Archäologie*, 1:237, 690; A. Bücheler, "Das Ausgiessen von Wein und Öl als Ehrung bei den Juden," *MGWJ* 49 (1905): 12–40; G. Dalman, *Arbeit und Sitte in Palästina* (Gütersloh, 1935), 4:259.

41. Lucian, *Life of Lucian* 11; *M. Šabbat* 23:5; the body is washed only in Acts 9:37. This occurrence is not mentioned in any of the Gospels in connection with Jesus' burial. In Mark 14:8, Jesus has interpreted the act of honor (14:3) as an embalming, *eis ton entaphiasmon;* thereby, he does not interpret it as the traditional washing and embalming of the body but as a special act of honoring the dead. One can conclude that because the especially expensive oil of nard (14:3) accompanies a very special act of *honor.*

42. Second Chron. 16:14; Josephus, *Ant.* 15.61; Plutarch, *Cato minor* 11; see the dousing of the grave with wine in Lucian, *Life of Lucian* 19; further material in Bücheler, "Das Ausgiessen," 29ff.; J. Marquardt, *Das Privatleben der Römer* (Leipzig, 1886), 1:368; L. Friedländer, *Darstellungen aus der Sittengeschichte Roms*, 10th ed. (Leipzig, 1922), 2:361; Dalman, *Arbeit und Sitte*, 4:264; Krauss, *Talmudische Archäologie*, 1:237; 2:60.

43. See Pliny the Elder, *Naturalis historia*, 12.42.
44. See Klostermann (*Das Markusevangelium*) on that passage; E. Haenchen, *Der Weg Jesu*, 2d ed. (Berlin, 1968), 541; Pesch, *Das Markusevangelium*, 529.
45. A. Lindemann, "Die Osterbotschaft des Markus: Zur theologischen Interpretation von Mark 16:1–8," *NTS* 26 (1980): 303.
46. It is called "gross forgetfulness" by H. Grass, *Ostergeschichten und Osterberichte*, 3d ed. (Göttingen, 1964), 20.
47. Ibid., 20; for methodologically similar explanations on 16:3–4, see Schenke, *Die Wundererzählungen*, 37; Pesch (*Das Markusevangelium*) says: "The question serves to prepare [the reader] for the miracle of the open door."
48. Bultmann says that verse 7 is a Markan ending; he says verse 8 is a pre-Markan ending that is, in light of 1 Cor. 15:3ff., a secondary apologetic legend, which is intended to explain why the fact that the tomb was empty became known so late; see R. Bultmann, *Die Geschichte der synoptischen Tradition*, 4th ed. (Göttingen, 1958), 308ff., and many others.
49. See, for example, the collection of material gathered by Pesch, *Das Markusevangelium*.
50. Lindemann ("Die Osterbotschaft," 305) notices correctly the arrangement of the text, in light of which *ouk estin hōde* does *not* mean *ēgerthē*, but that the empty grave is only a self-evident consequence of the resurrection. Then, one still would have to ask about the meaning of *ouk estin hōde*.... Pesch (*Das Markusevangelium*, 533) interprets verse 6 as a criticism of the women's behavior ("The search of the women... was directed... toward the dead person, whom they wanted to release to death through the body's embalming"), yet he then interprets the empty tomb as: Jesus was nowhere to be found. In reality, the text says that he can be found, namely in Galilee.
51. The phrases in 16:7 and 14:28 speak of the eschatological gathering of the scattered sheep of Mark 14:27; Zech. 13:7. A. Strobel's reference to Ezek. 34:13 makes good sense, even though *proagein* does not occur there (A. Strobel, "Der Berg der Offenbarung," in *Verborum Veritas* [Wuppertal, 1970], 145). Concerning the gathering of the scattered, see also Mark 13:27; Matt. 23:37 par. On the term *proagein*, see *poreuesthai opisō* (Luke 21:8); *deute opisō mou* (Mark 1:17); *erchesthai opisō* (Matt.

16:24); see also M. Hengel, *Nachfolge und Charisma* (Berlin, 1968), 24.

52. Hengel's hypothesis (in "Maria Magdalena") forms an exception; he assumes a first appearance to Mary Magdalene, which then is retouched by tradition.

53. Pesch (*Das Markusevangelium*, 536) tries to reinterpret the negative ending in Mark by religio-historical means; the parallel material he mentions—1 Sam. 3:15 (*Liber Antiquitatum Biblicarum* 53:12); Dan. 7:28; as well as the Markan commands to be silent—does not match the thought expressed in Mark 16:8 that an *order* given in the epiphany is *not followed*. Also, one cannot say that through Mark 16:8 the "role of the disciples as primary messengers of the resurrection" has been taken up in Mark. The disciples are still scattered when the Gospel ends. Also, they are not "primary messengers" to Mark (see above on 16:7). Hengel ("Maria Magdalena," esp. 253) has accurately emphasized the parallelism between the women (16:8) and the disciples; see also Broer, *Die Urgemeinde*, 108ff.

54. This has been stated particularly by E. Stegemann, *Das Markusevangelium*, 332–33.

55. I have tried to illustrate the historical connections in Schottroff, "Die Gegenwart."

56. W. Stegemann, "Lasset die Kinder zu mir kommen," in W. Schottroff and W. Stegemann, eds., *Traditionen der Befreiung* (Munich, 1980), 1:114–44; especially pp. 138–39 show that the "erosion of social ties" is an acute problem of the Markan community and results, ultimately, from the pressure of persecution.

57. On the fact that Matt. 28:10 is not only a repetition of Matt. 28:7 but has separate meaning, see especially K. Berger, *Die Auferstehung des Propheten und die Erhöhung des Menschensohnes* (Göttingen, 1976), 179, 467 n. 136, 498 n. 226. However, he misinterprets the role of Matt. 28:8–10 in its context when he says that "the purpose of this 'preliminary' appearance to the women" is to underline the credibility of the resurrection by making them "independent witnesses as distinguished from the disciples, though they are witnesses of secondary rank only" (p. 177).

58. J. Kremer, *Die Osterbotschaft der vier Evangelien*, 2d ed. (Stuttgart, 1968), 41.

59. The close connection between 28:1–10 and 28:16–20 is especially elaborated on by E. Lohmeyer, *Galiläa und Jerusalem* (Göttingen, 1936), 15–17.

60. With the use of *hoi de edistasan*, 28:8 shows, in comparison to 28:17, how easy it is for Matthew to depict the women as believers in contrast to "those of little faith" who can be found, of course, among both men and women. At any rate, he does not think that the contrast between Matt. 28:8 and 28:17 might be misinterpreted. The fact that they are women in 28:1–10 is not important to him; perhaps not even the term *opsontai* of 28:10 is important for him.

61. On the apocalyptic figure of the angel in Matt. 28:1–8, see Kremer, *Die Osterbotschaft*, 41–42; E. L. Bode, *The First Easter Morning* (Rome, 1970), 51; W. Trilling, *Christusverkündung in den synoptischen Evangelien* (Munich, 1969), 212ff.

62. It is neither historically nor theologically appropriate to conduct religio-psychological speculations on this aspect. After all, the truth of the women's faith in the risen one found expression in their actions.

63. See on that chap. 4, above.

64. See chap. 4, above.

Scripture Index

OLD TESTAMENT

Genesis
1:27	46
1:28	48, 97
16:1	159
17:17	159
17:19	159

Leviticus
15	145
15:15ff.	98
15:19–33	97

Deuteronomy
15:15	24
24:18	24
24:22	24

1 Samuel
1:1ff.	160
2:1–10	46, 160

2 Samuel
7	163

Nehemiah
5:1–5	22

Esther
1:9	70
2:3	70
2:14	70
4:13	70

Job
24:5	93
24:12	93
32:8	164
33:4	164

Psalms
33:6	164
37:12	172
104:30	164

Isaiah
9:5–10	163
61:1	24

Ezekiel
37:1–14	164

Daniel
7:14	163

Zechariah
13:7	185

NEW TESTAMENT

Matthew
1:18–25	158, 159
1:20	161
1:23	163, 190
1:25	161
5:1	170
5:3	24
5:3–4	25
5:9	27
5:44ff.	27
5:45	27
6:12	22
6:24	26
6:25–33	96
8:21	95
8:21–22	94
9:36	27
10:7–8	93
10:34–37	94, 95
11:1–5	92
11:2–5	93
11:5	25
13:55–57	159
14:21	170
14:33	190
14:35	170
15:38	170
17:26	25, 28
18:20	190
18:23–35	22
18:31	22
20:16	155, 178
21:31	97
21:31–32	151
21:35–36	22
22:6	22
23:37	94
24:9–14	189
24:37–39	94

24:51	22	9:6–7	95
25:40	170	9:23	28
26:31–35	190	9:31	185
26:32	190	9:35	177
26:56	190	9:36	177
26:69ff.	190	10:2–9	95–97, 194
27:55	190	10:5	96
27:55–56	91, 92	10:6–9	95
27:55–28:20	189–91	10:28	176
27:56	174	10:28–30	188
28:1	174	10:30	188
28:1–7	190	10:32	100, 178
28:1–8	191	10:32–34	178
28:1–20	190, 193	10:34	185
28:2	191	10:35–45	176
28:6	191	10:37	33
28:7	189, 190	10:42	22, 24
28:8	189, 190, 191	10:42–45	33, 95, 177
28:8–10	189, 190	10:43	33
28:8–19	186	10:45	177
28:9–10	35, 102	10:52	177
28:10	189, 190	13:10	187
28:16	190	13:11	32
28:16–20	186, 189, 190, 191	13:11–13	112
28:20	190	13:12	100
Mark		13:26–27	188
1:13	177	14:3	181
1:18	176	14:3–8	148
1:31	99, 176, 177	14:3–9	139
1:31c	177	14:8	181
1:45	177	14:17	187
3:6	173	14:27	185, 188
3:6–8	173, 179	14:28	183, 185, 187
3:31–35	95, 104	14:50	27, 100, 187
4:17	188	14:50–52	171
4:30–32	28	14:50–53	172
4:40	100	14:54	171, 172
5:20	177	14:66–72	172, 187
5:25–34	97–98	14:71	100
5:29	98	15:34	100
5:34	98	15:39	100
6:14–29	81, 82	15:40	98, 100, 101, 169–76, 178, 179, 191
6:44	170	15:40–41	91, 92, 99, 174
8:9	170	15:40–16:8	168–94
8:16	100	15:41	99, 169, 173, 176–78
8:17–20	185	15:41a	178
8:18	185	15:41b	178–79
8:31	185	15:47	100, 101, 173, 174, 175, 179–80
8:32	100	15:47–16:8	100, 101–2
8:34	176		
8:34–36	100		

Mark (continued)

16:1	100, 101, 173, 174, 175, 177, 180–82, 187
16:1–8	36, 101, 103, 179, 180, 183, 184, 185, 187, 193
16:2	181
16:3	182–83
16:3–4	182
16:4	183
16:5	183–84
16:6	183, 184–86, 185, 186
16:7	183, 184, 186–87
16:8	100–101, 104, 183, 184, 186, 187–89
16:10–11	103
16:12	103
16:14	103
23:49	179
27:55	179

Luke

1:7	159
1:11	159
1:19	159
1:24	160, 161
1:25	114
1:26	159–60, 162
1:26–28	161
1:26–38	158–65
1:27	159, 160–61
1:28	162
1:30	162
1:30–33	162–64
1:32	160
1:32ff.	163
1:35	161, 162, 164
1:36	160
1:37	160, 161
1:38	164–65
1:41	160
1:42	114
1:44	160
1:45	114
1:46–47	178
1:46–54	104, 163
1:46–55	46
1:48	162
1:53	93
1:60	114
2:19	114
2:36	114
3:23–28	160
4:18	162
6:20	170
6:20–21	93
7:36	140, 144
7:36–50	138–55
7:37	150, 151, 154
7:37ff.	151
7:37b	153–54
7:37b–38	153
7:38	154
7:39	140, 151
7:40	140
7:40–47	140
7:41–42	141, 143, 153
7:43	144
7:44	147
7:44–46	140
7:44–50	153
7:46	147, 154
7:47	150–51, 153
7:47b	141
8:1–3	91, 98
8:2	93, 139
8:3	92, 176
8:19–21	159
8:21	165
10:9	26
10:38–42	91, 114–15, 116, 117, 176, 194
10:39	114
10:40	114
10:41–42	116
11:26	115
11:27–28	114, 115, 116, 117, 194
11:28	116
12:37	178
12:45	22
12:58–59	22
13:18–19	163
14:15–24	141
14:26	91, 95
15:11–32	32
17:8	178
18:9–14	141, 142
18:11	147
18:14	147
18:29	91, 95
21:28	163
22:27	178
23:2	112
24:5–6	185

24:6	193
24:9–10	102
24:11	103, 193
24:20–21	103
24:21	193
24:24	103, 104
24:25–27	193

John

1:13	164
3:1–8	164
5:4	26
8:33	28
8:35	28
12:3ff.	181
19:39	181
20:6–8	102
20:18	102

Acts

1:8	179
1:14	62, 170
1:15	170
1:16	170
1:21–22	179
2:1ff.	164
2:13	31
2:17	31
2:42–47	26
4:31	32
5:14	170
8:3	170
8:12	170
9:1–19	183
9:2	170
9:36	114
9:36–40	114
9:43	134
10:6	134
12:12	62
13:14	65
13:50	61, 62–63, 64, 65, 67, 68
16:12–15	131–36
16:13	63, 64
16:13–14	62, 65, 67
16:13–24	64
16:13ff.	61
16:14	65
16:14–15	92
16:14–40	114
16:15	117
16:16–39	134
16:40	131
17:1–15	68
17:4	61, 62, 63, 64, 65, 67, 92
17:7–9	133
17:8	68
17:12	61, 62, 63, 65, 67, 68, 92
18:3	90
18:18	62
18:26	114
21:4	170
21:5	170
21:9	114

Romans

1:29–32	28
6:12–14	23
6:18–22	28
6:19	29
7:14–24	28–29
7:25	24
8	31
8:1	24
8:2	28
8:15–27	31
8:21	31
12:1–21	29
12:16	33
13:1–7	22, 111, 112
16	37, 106–8, 113
16:1–2	107
16:1–16	30
16:2	37
16:3	107
16:3–4	106
16:3–16	107, 108
16:4	37, 38, 107
16:6	38
16:7	36, 38, 106, 107, 108
16:8	107
16:9	107
16:10–11	106
16:12	38, 107
16:14–15	106
16:23	107

1 Corinthians

1:26–31	44
3:5	37
3:9	37
4:11–13	23
4:12	91
6:12	47

1 Corinthians (continued)

7	46–48
7:1	47
7:3–4	47
7:7	47
7:19	43
7:20	47
7:21	30
7:21–22	30
7:21ff.	23
7:22	44, 47
7:29	47, 48
7:29–35	47
7:32	47
7:33	47, 50
7:33–34	47
7:34	47
7:35	51
9:1	33
9:12	33
9:15	33
10:29	33
11:2–6	30
11:2–16	48–50, 51, 108, 111, 113
11:3	49, 50, 51, 108, 113
11:4	107
11:6	108
11:7–9	49
11:8	50
11:8–9	108
11:10	109, 110
11:11	49
11:11ff.	108
11:12	49, 50
11:13	108
11:14	49
11:14–15	108
11:16	51, 110, 113
12	33
12:3ff.	164
12:4–11	33
12:13	24, 31, 43
14:23	110
14:27ff.	50
14:29ff.	50
14:33	51
14:33b–36	50–51, 111
14:34ff.	111
14:40	51
15:3–8	35, 101, 102, 103
15:3ff.	179, 186, 189
16:16	38

Galatians

2:11ff.	44
3:26–28	43–46
3:28	24, 30, 40, 41, 44, 45, 46, 50, 52, 93, 108
3:28c	46
5:6	43
6:15	43

Ephesians

5:21–23	111

Philippians

1:1	107
4:2–3	37, 107
4:3	38

Colossians

3:11	43
3:18	111

1 Thessalonians

1:3	107
2:9	91

1 Timothy

2:1ff.	111
2:11–12	115
2:11–15	105, 111, 113
2:12–15	42
2:15	48
3:6ff.	111
5:3–16	111

2 Timothy

3:6	62
3:6–7	111

Titus

2:3–5	111
2:5	112
2:8	111
2:10	111

Philemon

16	44

1 Peter

3:1–6	111
3:1–7	111

www.ingramcontent.com/pod-product-compliance
Lightning Source LLC
Chambersburg PA
CBHW031245290426
44109CB00012B/447